THE END OF THE HOUSE OF WINDSOR

Other books by Stephen Haseler

The Gaitskellites
The Death of British Democracy
Eurocommunism (joint author)
The Tragedy of Labour
Anti-Americanism
The Battle For Britain: Thatcher and the New Liberals
The Politics of Giving

THE END OF THE HOUSE OF WINDSOR

Birth of a British Republic

Stephen Haseler

I.B.Tauris & Co Ltd
Publishers
London · New York

Published in 1993 by
I.B.Tauris & Co Ltd
45 Bloomsbury Square
London WC1A 2HY

A CIP record for this book is available from the British Library

ISBN 1-85043-735-1

Typeset by The Midlands Book Typesetting Company, Loughborough
Printed and bound in Great Britain by Heronsgate Ltd, Basildon, Essex
and WBC Ltd, Bridgend, Mid Glamorgan

Contents

v

Picture sources

The author and publisher are grateful to the following for permission to reproduce pictures:

1, Tim Graham; 2, National Portrait Gallery, London; 3, (above left and right) National Portrait Gallery, (below) Hulton Deutsch Collection; 4, National Portrait Gallery; 5, Cecil Beaton/Camera Press; 6, (below) Planet News; 7, Camera Press/Imperial War Museum, London; 8 & 9, Hulton Deutsch Collection; 10, Cecil Beaton/Camera Press; 11, National Portrait Gallery; 12, Camera Press; 13, Tim Graham; 14, Popperfoto; 15, Pitkin; 16, Godfrey Argent; 18, 19, 20, 21 & 22, Tim Graham; 23, Melanie Friend/Format Photographers; 24, Tim Graham; 25, City Museum and Art Gallery, Birmingham; 26, (below) National Portrait Gallery; 27, Leeds City Council; 28, Hulton Deutsch Collection; 29, (above) Rex Features, (below) Tim Graham; 30, Tim Graham; 31, *Daily Mirror*; 32, Rex Features.

Every effort has been made to trace copyright holders, and we apologise in advance for any unintentional omission. Any error will be rectified in subsequent editions of the book.

Introduction

The wedding of Charles and Diana on 29 July 1981 was the high-water mark of the House of Windsor's public relations campaign to reconcile the British monarchy with the democratic (and television) age by associating itself with the family, and with family values. Charles and Diana followed Elizabeth and Philip in the projection of the royal house as essentially a family institution – indeed as the ideal family. And they did it superbly. Who then would have predicted that, only twelve years later, the British monarchy's fortunes would have declined so far that its very future might rest upon what by then had become the fragile marriage of a fairy-tale princess and her Prince Charming? Who would have believed that Diana Spencer, the seemingly shy and dutiful new princess, was to become such a pivotal figure in the drama? Of course, the monarchy's contradictions would have caught up with it sooner or later. Yet it is Princess Diana who – because of her popularity and her refusal to play the royal game – has, perhaps unwittingly, precipitated a crisis in the constitution.

It is fitting that the travails of Diana's and Charles's marriage should be the catalyst for major change. This 'love match of the century' was always a joke. But the joke was upon the British people, perfectly representing the manipulative ability of the royal family and its public relations machine as it played upon the public's illusions and fantasies, not only about the

1

couple themselves, but about their country too. Now that the public relations veil is stripped aside, and light has been let in on magic, the standing of Britain's monarchy has undergone a transformation.

The monarchy is a personal institution, and therefore rides and falls on the attributes, quirks and deficiencies of individuals – and in the Windsors' case upon the family. In 1952, when Elizabeth Windsor returned from Africa having ascended to the throne upon the death of her father, her position seemed impregnable. Forty years later, by the beginning of 1993, the House of Windsor had become a laughing stock. The idealised dream family of the 1950s and 1960s had collapsed. Her sister, her daughter and two of her sons all seemed incapable of sustaining marriages with what commentators still cutely describe as 'commoners', while the troubled life of Princess Diana so awakened the public's sympathy that it appeared to induce a popular conception of the royal family as stiff, cold, remote and deeply archaic. Even the Queen was looking less than dignified. Her initial refusal to pay any taxes at all, together with her later decision (taken after considerable pressure) to pay *some* taxes, exposed a surprisingly wilful streak, an unedifying stubbornness in the royal personality. The hasty decision of the government to pay for the damage caused by the Windsor Castle fire revealed the extent to which the Queen and her family live at public expense – more lavishly than any other comparable head of state, including the American president (who not only represents a superpower but also carries on the duties of a chief executive).

These personal issues of marriage, fidelity, lifestyle and taxes inevitably affected the standing of the personal institution of the monarchy. By 1993 the question of whether the monarchy was relevant to the needs of the country as it approached a new millennium had become an issue on the political agenda. The prospect of a reign of Charles III seemed improbable. And the idea – floated by desperate monarchists – that upon the Queen's death or abdication the House of Windsor, in order to save itself, should skip a generation (and hand the throne to William) seemed contrived. The Queen herself contributed to the growing sense of crisis in the House of Windsor by her '*annus horribilis*' remarks in late 1992. Normally quite politically astute, the Queen displayed a degree of insensitivity by calling attention – in front of a national audience of millions of families in dire economic straits – to her own trials and tribulations; her somewhat pleading tone only legitimised the idea of a monarchy under siege.

By February 1993, the popularity of the monarchy had plummeted. A Gallup survey revealed that a staggeringly low 26 per cent of those polled thought the 'monarchy something to be proud of'.[1] And on 23 February 1993 the Australian Prime Minister announced that his Party, should it win the general election, would call a referendum to abolish the monarchy and establish a federal republic. And so talk increasingly turned not only to reforming the monarchy, but also to the possibility of a republic in Britain.

What emerged out of the great 'royal debate' was that the British monarchy was a very important institution indeed, certainly not the inconsequential trifle which pro-monarchists tended to suggest it was, as a means of deflecting criticism. The narrow, upper-crust life of the royals (a caricature of unearned privilege, particularly sharply focused in a country in recession) is symbolic of Britain's continuing class problem. And, more importantly still, the institution of monarchy hurts the country by reinforcing Britain's inability to break with its imperial past, and the destructive sense of over-importance which went with it. The monarchy was also the apex of a very outdated constitutional system, an *ancien régime* of truly antique proportions. All in all, the monarchy perpetuates a culture of backwardness in a nation desperately needing to modernise itself, and thus may have a bearing on the future prosperity and security of the peoples of Britain.

The dawning truth about Britain in the post-war period is that the country seems to be running out of options. We have tried virtually every economic strategy for revival. We have seen a Keynesian welfare state constructed by a seemingly all-embracing post-war political consensus. We have also witnessed its overthrow and replacement by the neo-liberal economic regime of Thatcherism. We have seen fixed rates of exchange and floating rates of exchange, lax monetary targets and tight monetary targets, 'tax and spend' fiscal policies and low-tax, balanced-budget regimes. No matter what the economic regime, the relative decline of the British economy (and with it Britain's political position in Europe and the world) has continued apace.

This bleak record has one advantage: it is now clear (and more acceptable to propose) that Britain's problem is not primarily one of finding the technically correct economic policy and strategy. After all, the West's more successful economies and societies provide distinct economic models of development. For example, the United States is classically capitalist and individualist in its approach, and post-war Germany more *dirigiste* and corporatist. *Both* are more successful than Britain. The lesson is obvious. Although the debate about economic policy will continue, it can be no substitute for addressing more profound problems at the heart of the modern British experience – problems located in the very culture of the country.

This book suggests that our culture – the way we think, the way we talk, the values we live by, indeed 'the British way of life' – no longer allows us to compete effectively in the modern commercial world. I shall also argue that in modern Britain a residual, but still powerful, jingoism (based upon a largely uneducated and provincial sensibility) reinforces this deadly cultural conservatism, preventing the country from fully modernising itself – and from taking advantage of the new global economy and the integration of Europe.

Thus I argue for what amounts to a cultural revolution, an overhaul not just of Britain's institutions but also of our values, of the way we think about ourselves, of our attitudes to foreigners and the wider world. There is no magic wand that will turn modern Britons into an outward-looking, confident and competitive people. Nor should there be. Yet one thing that people and politicians can do – and can do fairly quickly, should they put their mind to it – is reform and change the institutions and constitutions (the framework and symbolism of political life) that govern them. My argument here is that, over time, new attitudes and aspirations would follow.

4

What is needed, as we approach a radically new involvement in Europe, is a fundamental change in our system of government. Britain's royal-state – with its unwritten constitution and its tightly drawn network of monarchy, Lords, and established Church – is not only a constitutional anachronism; it also represents, reflects and encourages a series of attitudes which hobble the country's development.

The British, obviously increasingly ill at ease with their failing constitutional monarchy, must resist the temptation simply to tinker with what is a fundamentally flawed system of governance. Indeed, it is just such tinkering, such last-minute 'Band aid' politics, which has produced our present travails. Instead, we need to seize the hour, to take advantage of the new era presented by a new European adventure and take up where we left off in the 1640s, establishing ourselves as a republic.

A republican system of government amounts, of course, to a precise set of rules (which I attempt to set out in Chapter 10). At the same time, it represents a set of republican virtues, a deeper notion of how people in civil society should relate to one another, a modern democratic republic encouraging democratic manners. Who can seriously doubt that, say, twenty years on from the end of our *ancien régime*, the British, whatever else they will be, will be a less deferential, less tradition-mired, less class-conscious, and a less nostalgic people – a people more attuned to change and survival?

The view that there is some kind of link between constitution and culture, and between culture and economic performance, has for many decades, and certainly during the lifetime of this author, been dismissed and marginalised. Only now is it beginning to be seen as something of an orthodoxy – indeed, a consensus. Constitutional change is now established on the agenda of British politics, and increasingly the issue of the monarchy is seen as one of the major obstacles to such change; as this book goes to press, we are witnessing the first serious parliamentary criticism of the monarchy for a generation and more.

More crucially still, a new consensus seems to be forming around the idea that the culture of monarchy stands in the way of creating an open, democratic society. Many left-wing politicians and commentators are critical of the monarchy for its role in perpetuating a class system that inhibits democratic change, while modern Conservatives are coming to see it as inhibiting the creation of an 'enterprise culture'; equally, Britain's growing constitutional reform movement – including the influential Charter 88 – increasingly views the monarchy as a legitimate item on its agenda for change. Even Margaret Thatcher is reported as having severe misgivings about the monarchy.[2]

The fall of the House of Windsor in public esteem may have been precipitated by the personal family problems which have been given so much publicity. Yet independently of what happened in the royal house, Britain was going to have to decide its future direction – whether to become a truly modern nation or, alternatively, to lapse into a kind of offshore Ruritanian fantasy land. Britain has chosen to reassess itself, and the family problems of the Windsors have become the excuse, not the occasion, for a review of the monarchy.

No doubt, in time-honoured tradition, the royal-state will attempt a compromise. At some point the British people will be offered 'the Scandinavian option' – a British monarchy cut down to Norwegian, Danish or Swedish size.[3] This option (which, incidentally, includes the non-Scandinavian, bicycle-riding Dutch royals) is, however, quite radical, and will only be attempted when things are very desperate indeed. The Swedes, Norwegians and Danes all have written constitutions; they all have abolished their upper houses based upon nobility (the Danes abolished their upper house, the Landsting, in 1949, at the same time as they provided for female succession to the throne); they all practise the separation of Church and state; and the functions of their monarchies are purely ceremonial – and the ceremonies, by Windsor standards, are relatively simple. These monarchies exude a wholesome simplicity which contrasts strongly with the culture of deference, obsequiousness, patronage and class privilege that characterises the British model. The Swedish monarchy, for example, since the new constitution of 1974, is devoid of prerogative powers; and the royal house of King Carl Gustaf XVI and Queen Silvia exists under a written constitution in which 'all public power in Sweden emanates from the people'.[4]

To describe this Scandinavian model is to appreciate why it cannot work in Britain, where the monarchy is essentially an either/or phenomenon. It is *either* the present lavish, intrusive political animal with its worldwide public relations appeal and soap opera status – *or* it is nothing. Any attempt to reform it along Scandinavian lines will be doomed. For a start, such a transformation from the present encrusted royal behemoth would signify nothing less than the final defeat of the House of Windsor; like the Commonwealth set up in the 1950s as a sop to the former Empire, such a 'bicycling monarchy' would only be, could only be, a stop-gap measure, engineered in order to mollify the susceptibilities of the royal family. The arguments of republicans would have been humiliatingly conceded, leading inevitably to demands that the country might as well go the whole way.

For some, the death of the British royal-state will be a time for sadness, for lamentation, for evoking the sensibilities which respond to the idea of a 'thousand years of history'. For others, it means an opportunity, a blessed relief from the seemingly endless constrictions imposed upon the British people by a failed state, its narrow culture and its undemocratic and socially remote elite.

This royal-state can best be summed up as representing a combination of heavy feudal ideology and symbolism, together with an over-mighty executive. Its institutions are tightly interconnected. Abolish or reform one, and the whole lot comes into question. For instance, should the House of Lords be abolished (or reformed to include only elected persons), then the monarchy (which is also based upon the hereditary principle) would be brought into question, and the established Church would lose a major aspect of its establishment – its bishops in the legislature. Introduce a major constitutional innovation like an entrenched Bill of Rights, and the whole structure is threatened. For instance, an entrenched Bill of Rights would need a written constitution which, in turn, would need to define and limit all institutions, and thus would bring into question not only the monarchy, the Lords and the established Church, but would also destroy the 'sovereignty' of the 'Queen in Parliament' and change the role of the courts (by establishing a constitutional court).

The death of the royal-state, as it merges with, and then is submerged within, the new structures of Europe, will be a liberating experience for the British people. This 'United Kingdom' has controlled and limited (indeed, stunted) the development and aspirations of the people of these islands for too long. It has helped to breed all the characteristics of what is still the 'British disease'. Above all, its culture of paternalism has denied its people the rights and responsibilities of citizenship. In the United Kingdom, all are subjects.

In this book I argue that the British are already over half-way towards establishing a republican form of government. We increasingly believe in most of the republican virtues, and we now possess – through the European union – a continent-wide republican framework. A British republic could come about by a single Act of Parliament disestablishing the monarchy, and voted upon in a subsequent referendum.

I should like to thank my friends in Republic (particularly that indefatigable republican advocate Dr Edgar Wilson) and in the Radical Society who have encouraged me to write this book. A debt of gratitude is also due both to the assiduous editorial team at I.B.Tauris and to colleagues in my department at the London Guildhall University who helped me to refine many of the arguments.

Stephen Haseler
London, March 1993

8

1· Whatever Happened to 'The Good Old Cause'?

Britain became a republic on 17 February 1649. Eleven years later, with Oliver Cromwell safely dead, the royal-state reasserted itself. And ever since, the idea of monarchy – whether informed by 'divine right' or limited by a 'constitutional monarchy' – has guided and informed the structures of the English, and then the British, state.

What, in these intervening years, happened to the republican cause in its struggle against the arbitrary authority of the royal-state?

Of course, the English of the seventeenth century were among the first republicans of the modern age. The republic established by the parliamentary forces which defeated Charles I in the civil war, though called a 'Commonwealth' (a term now used by Tony Benn in his 1992 republican Commonwealth of Britain Bill), lacked many of the modern republican virtues and soon relapsed into what amounted to a quasi-monarchical system. Yet as Christopher Hill has argued, 'the seventeenth is the decisive century in English history, the epoch in which the Middle Ages ended';[1] and the revolution, a progressive leap forward if ever there was one, destroyed royal absolutism even if it did not introduce a republican constitutional settlement.

Perhaps this republican eruption came too early in the nation's history; perhaps, had it occurred later, say at the time of the American and French revolutions, the social and political environment might have been ripe enough to turn republican sentiment into a republican constitution which could last. But in any event, Cromwell's revolution did unleash a republican impulse which, although it was to spend much of its time underground, or as part of a broader Whig and Liberal radicalism, nonetheless became a serious strand of British political thought. Systematic republicanism started with the republican groups of the civil war, led by such figures as Henry Marten, Edmund Ludlow, Henry Neville and the 'democratic republicans',[2] John Lilburne, Richard Overton and William Walwyn, and came to inspire some of the country's greatest poets and theorists – Milton, Blake, Shelley, Locke, Thackeray and H. G. Wells among them. It was Milton, supporter of the regicide and the republic which followed it, who gave initial voice to 'The Good Old Cause' of English republicanism and who was the 'last significant figure to defend "The Good Old Cause" in April 1660, a few weeks before Charles II returned':[3]

> What I have spoken is the language of that which is not called amiss 'The Good Old Cause' ... Thus much I should perhaps have said though I were sure I should have spoken only to trees and stones; and had none to cry to but with the Prophet, 'O earth, earth, earth!' to tell the very soil itself what her perverse inhabitants are deaf to. Nay, though what I have spoke should happen (which Thou suffer not, who didst create mankind free; nor Thou next, who didst redeem us from being servants of men!) to be the last words of our expiring liberty. But I trust I shall have spoken persuasion to abundance of sensible and ingenious men; to some perhaps whom God may raise of these stones to become children of reviving liberty.[4]

Liberty did not 'expire', and the 'children of reviving liberty' were to be plentiful and influential. The political theorist John Locke started to 'revive liberty' with his late seventeenth-century anti-Stuart treatises.[5] He, and other republicans such as Algernon Sidney, James Harrington and Henry Neville, were

10

often able to square their republicanism with the existence of a king (whom, very radically for their day, they wished to see elected, rather like a president). The era inaugurated by the 1688 constitutional settlement, with its reaffirmation of monarchy, meant that republicanism would need to become more theoretical and less precise and overt. Monarchy as such ceased to be the central issue; rather, it came to represent and symbolise the executive role in the state, perhaps to be elected, perhaps to be limited and constrained by Parliament.

There is little doubt that the 'Glorious Revolution' of 1688 was a major setback for republican and radical thinking in Britain. Certainly the historian J. H. Plumb, who describes what happened then as the 'triumph of the Venetian oligarchy', sees it as such:

> The seventeenth century had witnessed the beginnings and partial success of a bourgeois revolution that came near to changing the institutions of government. In this, however, it never succeeded. The revolution of 1688 and all that followed were retrogressive from the point of view of the emergence into political power. Socially and economically they continued to thrive, but not politically.[6]

Without a bourgeois revolution, there could be no serious republican agitation or activity. However, republican ideas continued to inform both Whigs and radicals. Whigs had portraits of Oliver Cromwell in their homes in the second decade of the eighteenth century; and Shelburne could argue at that century's end that, during the republic, 'talents of every kind began to show themselves, which were immediately crushed or put to sleep at the restoration'.[7]

The late eighteenth century was to see the emergence of the dominating figure of English radicalism, Tom Paine. This son of an East Anglian staymaker, who became a Sussex customs official, was to become England's premier republican and, though pilloried at home, was to influence and take part in the two great revolutions of the modern world. Paine's *Rights of Man* (1792) and *Common Sense* (1776) are two of the great polemical works of English liberalism. His republicanism was uncompromising. In those forensic tones that were to annoy so many in the English establishment of his day, he argued that a monarch was 'as absurd as an hereditary mathematician, or an hereditary wiseman, and as ridiculous as an hereditary poet laureate'.[8] Paine, however, was the classic case of a man out of joint with his times – with British-time, that is, not world-time! He was recognised in both the United States and France as a key intellectual influence upon their democratic revolutions, yet it has taken two centuries for his reputation to be revived in the land of his birth.

Tom Paine's reputation is now being resurrected in Britain. A statue of him has been erected in his native Norfolk; a tree was recently dedicated to him in Buckinghamshire; Margaret Thatcher included quotes from him in her speeches; learned works about him are beginning to appear again, the most recent by the philosopher A. J. Ayer; his collected works are reprinted; his *Rights of Man*, and the example of his turbulent life of principle, continues to inspire both constitutional reformism and contemporary republicanism. In 1988 Professor David Marquand described Tom Paine as 'the embodiment, symbol and shaper of a tradition of British popular radicalism which has gone underground for most of the twentieth century but which may well hold the key to the politics of the next'.[9]

Paine's great adversary, the Irish Whig Edmund Burke, succeeded in marginalising not only Paine but also republican and radical sentiment in Britain, by turning fears about the excesses of the French Revolution against the principles for which it (together with the American revolution, and indeed English liberalism more generally) stood. He gave English Tories the justification they were seeking for the protection of their peculiarly undemocratic institutions. He was monarchy's great friend, and in his battle with Tom Paine (one of the great bouts of all time) he won all the early and middle rounds, and only now looks as though he may be knocked out in the tenth.

In the early part of the nineteenth century radical campaigning concentrated upon such issues as extending the franchise and reforming Parliament – culminating in the Chartist movement. However, republican ideas were never far below the surface. The works of a generation of men of letters – including Wordsworth, Coleridge, Blake, Hardy, Shelley and Byron – were replete with republican themes. Wordsworth declared: 'The office of King is a trial to which human virtue is not equal. Pure and universal representation, by which alone liberty can be secured, cannot, I think, exist together with monarchy.'[10] And in an age when punches were not pulled, Byron talked of 'royal vampires' (in his poem 'Windsor Poetics', 1814) and Shelley of 'Kings and parasites' (in his poem 'Kings and Parasites', 1812). Republican themes were also present in the works and activities of William Cobbett, Robert Owen, Samuel Bamford, William Hazlitt, John Clare, and many of those involved with the Chartist movement.

By the mid- to late nineteenth century, republicanism was virtually received wisdom among many educated middle-class Englishmen. Dickens, with his acerbic attacks upon aristocrats ('Lord Coodle', 'Sir Thomas Doodle' and 'the Duke of Foodle'), and Thackeray (particularly following his 1856 course of lectures highly critical of 'The Four Georges') contributed to republican sentiment. And the philosophers of liberalism – such as Jeremy Bentham and John Stuart Mill – also advanced republican ideas, normally placing them in the context of scepticism about executive authority. Witness John Stuart Mill in 1861:

> It has long (perhaps throughout the entire duration of British freedom) been a common saying, that if a good despot could be ensured, despotic monarchy would be the best form of government. I look upon this as a radical and most pernicious misconception of what good government is; which, until it can be got rid of, will fatally vitiate all our speculations on government.[11]

Mill was the nineteenth-century middle-class liberal *par excellence*, and typical too of a frame of mind which would have professed republican sympathies. He had little concern for, or need to emulate, the aristocracy; and at the same time possessed little sympathy for either working-class deference or trade unionism. Indeed, in the century following Mill's *On Liberty*, had his bourgeois approach not been squeezed out of British politics by a middle class infatuated with land and court and a working class mired in tradition, then republicanism might even have prevailed during his century.

Republicanism nearly coalesced into a real threat to the royal-state in the 1870s. Anti-monarchist sentiment, which during the late 1860s had been on the increase – the result of public disenchantment with Queen Victoria's absence from public life, and resentment at what was seen as her extravagant financial demands upon Parliament – translated itself into republican activity as republican clubs sprang up throughout the country.[12] In April 1871 a large trade-union-based demonstration against the monarchy was staged in Hyde Park, and later that same year, in July, George Dangerfield reported that:

> the public resentment at length came to a head, when a great mass meeting submerged the fountains and the lions in Trafalgar Square and flowed from the steps of St. Martin's Church to the entrance to the barracks. Here Charles Bradlaugh – it was just a week after the Queen had asked Parliament for some provision for her son Arthur – protested against 'any more grants to princely paupers' and shouted that the House of Brunswick should take warning, for the patience of the English public was almost exhausted.[13]

There was rarely anything particularly stately about these outbursts of republicanism. In November 1871, at a republican meeting in Bolton, tempers became so frayed that the meeting dissolved, breaking into a pitched battle in which a republican, William Schofield, was killed by a stone-throwing, pro-monarchist mob.

By 1873 a national Republican League was launched at a conference in Birmingham, and one of the country's leading radicals, the secular humanist Charles Bradlaugh, became its president.[14] A flavour of the strong emotions and strong words of the time is captured by a speech given to the Manchester Republican Club by Richard Pankhurst in 1873:

> It is not so much the direct power of the Crown which is so injurious, as its indirect influence. It is the shelter of privilege, the centre of vested and sinister influences. It is the excuse for receiving large emoluments without rendering any service . . . the lineal descendants of the despotic sovereign and the tyrannic nobility are the Crown . . . and the hereditary peerage sitting in the House of Lords.[15]

Senior elected politicians also got caught up in the excitement, and began to raise the issue of republicanism in the formal arenas of politics. The most committed to 'The Good Old Cause' was Sir Charles Dilke, whose short campaign against the monarchy tended to rest upon its financial profligacy. He demanded a parliamentary inquiry into royal expenses; and Victoria considered him such a threat to the monarchy that she successfully lobbied Gladstone to deny him serious office.

Joe Chamberlain, 'Radical Joe', was another overt republican, although in his case this was less a principled than a 'political' act, as he was obviously toying with using anti-monarchist sentiment as a means of furthering his career. 'I have been taxed with professing Republicanism', he stated in a speech in early December 1872, and: 'I hold, and very few intelligent people do not now hold, that the best form of government for a free and enlightened people is that of a Republic, and that is the form of government to which the nations of Europe are surely and not very slowly tending.'[16] Yet Chamberlain was not to develop a campaign, and instead pledged himself against 'agitation' on the issue.

This rush of republicanism in the 1870s was, in part, caused by developments in Europe. Public opinion had sided with France (*republican* France) in the Franco-Prussian War, and against the victorious Germans – and by extension against the German Queen, Victoria. Among certain sections of opinion the French reforms of 1870 may also have had a knock-on effect.[17] There was also, however, the raw issue of money. Victoria's demands on Parliament for extra state cash highlighted what had, in fact, been a running sore for most of her reign. In the early part of the century Richard Carlisle, Paine's printer and editor of the *Republican*, had depicted the monarchy as 'a profligate consumer of the nation's wealth'.[18] And at the century's end the radical Labouchere argued in an article in the *Fortnightly Review*: 'Radicals are essentially practical . . . Their objection to the present state of things is mainly based upon financial grounds. Admitting that there is to be a hereditary figurehead, they cannot understand why it should cost so much.'[19]

What remains so startling about this outburst of nineteenth-century republicanism was how seriously it was taken, not only by Buckingham Palace, but also by the Party leaders. Of course, it was not the extent of republicanism that worried the establishment, but rather its potential for rapid, engulfing growth. Gladstone, Disraeli and the Queen were all in on an attempted construction of a royal-state that would carry Britain into the next century; they had, no doubt, imbibed Walter Bagehot's warning about letting republican 'light' in on royal 'mystery', and Gladstone, for one, was determined not only to limit republican sentiment, but to expunge it altogether. In a ruthless memo to his Queen about how she could use ceremonials to improve her position, he argued:

> What we should look to was not merely meeting [republicanism] by a more powerful display of opposite emotions, but to getting rid of it altogether, for it could never be satisfactory that there should exist even a fraction of the nation republican in its views. To do this it would be requisite to consider every mode in which this great occasion [the Thanksgiving Service for the Prince of Wales's recovery] could be turned to account . . .[20]

Organised republicanism in late-nineteenth-century Britain was ultimately, however, insubstantial, and when at the end of November 1871 the Prince of Wales fell ill with typhoid fever, this was all that was needed to prick the republican bubble.

Radical sentiment, which at the beginning of the century had been directed away from republicanism towards Chartism was now redirected towards trade union organisation for manual workers, and, for the middle class, towards socialism. Thus the royal-state sailed on, and republicanism became, in Nairn's view, 'little more than a vandalising impulse, taboo-shrunk to mere naughtiness: unable to upset the landscape'; the former rebels were 'reduced to stealing papa's stamp album or carving their initials on the ancestral furniture'.[21]

Indeed, for most of the twentieth century – until the re-awakening of republicanism in the 1990s – dissenters have not even felt able to carve their initials on the furniture. So total was the consensus created by the late-nineteenth-century royal myth-makers – with their magical mix of Empire, deference and ceremonial – that what republican sympathies existed went underground. There is no way of telling how many secretly harboured republican thoughts. Certainly any serious radical or liberal, no matter what their personal beliefs, would not have thought it worth the candle to raise the republican standard. Roy Jenkins, then a Labour MP, perhaps referring to his own career and those of others of his generation, argued that Joe Chamberlain 'realised that to link the fortunes of British radicalism with those of British republicanism would be to deliver a damaging and unnecessary blow to the former cause'.[22]

Inevitably, there were powerful republican undertones swirling around the great debate over the House of Lords which led up to the Parliament Act in 1911. Indeed, a reading of the preamble to the Act, which stated that it was intended to 'reconstitute the House of Lords on a popular basis instead of a hereditary basis', should have sent shivers down the spine of any courtier with half an understanding of the meaning of words.[23] Yet neither Asquith nor Lloyd George (for all his anti-aristocratic rhetoric) felt able to add the monarchy to their radical prospectus.

As Labour replaced the Liberals, and the thrust of left-wing radicalism switched from attacks upon the constitution of the landed interest to a critique of capitalism and industry, so the republican cause faced another setback. There was still some minor republican agitation – in the early 1920s, the issue of monarchy was debated by the Labour Party, even formally in one of its annual conferences – but the Party leaders, including its left-wing saint, George Lansbury, successfully sidestepped the issue. Republicanism became 'the dog that never barked'.[24]

The attitude towards monarchy of Clement Attlee, Labour's post-war Prime Minister, is revealing. In May 1936 the Labour Party had opposed the civil list estimates, but Attlee, then Opposition leader, rushed to explain that 'there is no suggestion in our opposition of republicanism or of opposition to monarchy . . . I would not raise a finger to turn a capitalist monarchy into a capitalist republic.'[25] While critical of the snobbery that surrounded the monarchy, and 'the continual round of obsequiousness', he nonetheless rounded on the republican agitation of the 1870s, declaring it to have been fomented not by socialists but rather by dreaded 'bourgeois radicals'. Labour was thus to remain 'lousy but loyal' for some time longer.

In 1931 Harold Laski, Professor of Political Science at the London School of Economics, issued a direct attack upon the King for interfering (in what he argued amounted to a 'Palace Revolution') in the political crisis of that year; he suggested that Ramsay MacDonald had become Prime Minister only because he was 'the King's favourite'.[26] Apart from this attempt to scratch the 'ancestral furniture', however, for the next thirty years or so, under the impact of war and post-war rebuilding, the monarchy simply died as a radical issue. There were hints of republicanism in Tony Benn's campaign against the House of Lords in the late 1950s, and Richard Crossman's in the late 1960s, and again in Benn's attempt, while Postmaster General in the Wilson government, to remove the Queen's head from some British stamps. Yet the anti-monarchist campaign of moderate Labour MP Willie Hamilton received no support from his own Party leadership or any major Party faction. (In his memoirs, *Blood on the Walls*, Hamilton writes that in the early 1980s he proposed in a memorandum to Labour's National Executive that the Queen and employees of the Crown be given the status equivalent to civil servants under a new

18

royal department of state with its own government minister; these proposals were not acted upon). Even as I write, the Labour Party has not formally debated the issue of monarchy – although leading Labour figures like Roy Hattersley, Jack Straw and Marjorie Mowlem have been publicly critical of the royal institution.

Beyond politics, in the literary establishment, the taboo reigned well into the 1980s. When Piers Brendon published the republican book *Our Own Dear Queen* in 1986, it was largely ignored by the critics, and the author was booed on the *Wogan* show on television. Two years previously, the *Observer* had not only commissioned, but accepted, a republican article from Brendon, which they finally refused to publish.[27] But it was to be only a few years before the intellectual tide turned somewhat, and a growing republicanism among opinion-formers was further boosted by Tom Nairn's *The Enchanted Glass* (1988) and Edgar Wilson's *The Myth Of British Monarchy* (1989).

When opinion did finally turn against the British monarchy in the 1990s, it did so with a vengeance. Almost overnight – seemingly – parliamentary opinion broke free of the royal spell. Although the standard syrup from the Party leaders accompanied the 1992 announcement by the Prime Minister that the Prince and Princess of Wales had separated, the convention that the House of Commons did not discuss royalty was broken as, for the first time, criticism of the monarchy – and calls for a republic – echoed from the Commons floor. In early 1993 a poll announced that nearly a quarter of Labour MPs were in favour of 'Britain becoming a republic', and republican noises were also heard within the Conservative Party, from voices as distinct as those of George Walden and Anthony Beaumont Dark.[28] Furthermore the last decade of the century has witnessed the growth of a systematic republicanism within the body politic of the dying royal-state. Liberal Democrat Simon Hughes – whose Private Member's Bill would have *compelled* the Queen to pay tax before she volunteered to pay *some* – and that formidable old radical Tony Benn, with his comprehensive republican Commonwealth of Britain Bill, may represent the tip of an iceberg, suggesting a potential coalition which might, in place of royal-bashing, produce the republican alternative. Should that happen, then the statue of our chief man of liberty Oliver Cromwell, which stands outside the Houses of Parliament, may finally be seen to possess some meaning.

2·The Crisis of the Royal-state

The extent of the royal-state

The British state is one of a handful of monarchies still standing in the late twentieth century. It is a royal-state in the sense that its head – Queen Elizabeth II – derives her position solely from the attribute of heredity; she is a member of a 'royal' family from which successors and heirs of the king or queen are drawn. This primitive, tribal idea of kingship still infuses Britain's (unwritten) constitution; yet the country has evolved into what is now, technically, a 'constitutional monarchy' – the term used to describe the legal relationship of monarch to state in which the 'sovereign' is no longer absolute (in the sense of drawing legitimacy from the idea of rule by divine right) but exists within the framework of law and constitution.

The term 'constitutional monarchy' evokes – strangely for Britain – an image of modernity in which the British state is 'sold' by its supporters as really quite like all modern systems, including republican ones; the 'monarchy' aspect becomes but a harmless frivolity, a historical icing on the cake. This view of the British royal-state has been implicit in the works of an array of scholars and thinkers dating back to the mid-nineteenth century, when Walter Bagehot burst on the scene with his great gift to monarchy, *The English Constitution* (1867).

21

Bagehot, by creating the idea that monarchy was the 'dig-nified' part of the British constitution, both re-created a role for it and, at the very same time, provided, in Tom Nairn's words, an 'alibi for not bothering to think farther about it'. Nairn suggests that since 1867 'almost everyone has picked up this alibi and used it'.[1] Such is certainly the case with the great nineteenth-century constitutional scholar Albert Venn Dicey (who formulated the constitutional notion of 'The Crown in Parliament'). Twentieth-century constitutionalists such as Sir Ivor Jennings, Professor Hood Phillips, Sir Kenneth Weare and Professor Philip Norton have all reinforced the Bagehotian *mot*: that serious students of politics should direct themselves, not at the role of the monarchy, but rather at the concept of the sovereignty of Parliament.

This received idea is flawed. In fact, not only does monarchy sit at the very heart of the British state, but, more importantly, it dominates its political, cultural and economic reach. Friedrich Engels, in his mid-nineteenth-century survey *The Condition of the Working Class in England*, captured the point when he argued: 'Remove the Crown, the "subjective apex", and the whole artificial structure comes tumbling down . . . And the less important the monarchic element became in reality, the more important did it become for the Englishman.'[2]

Intriguingly, Bagehot, somewhat contradicting his skilful marginalising of the monarchy, agreed with Engels. Speaking of Queen Victoria, he asserted grandly that 'without her in England the present English government would fail and pass away'.[3]

In fact the modern British state is really a royalist state, in the sense that the existence of monarchy is not a random throw of history, nor a constitutional quirk; rather, monarchy, 'the Crown' and 'royal' mean much more than might be supposed by, say, a Scandinavian understanding of modern monarchy – a fact demonstrated by the very powerful idea of heredity which permeates British life: the royal-state possesses a legislative branch in which heredity is a qualification for office, and continues with a legal notion of primogeniture in which rights of succession pass to the first-born male. All this in a wider culture in which heredity, particularly as it relates to land, holds powerful sway. Furthermore, the role of the monarchy is crucial in legitimising the state. For the British, the Crown *is* the state: state and monarchy are fused.

The recognisable features of the English state (of the 'thousand years of history') probably started some time in the tenth century – at the very time when the English established their monarchy. And no surprise this, for it was the impress of monarchy which gave to England (and many other 'nations') its first sense of an ordered political organisation. Thus we might intone, 'In the beginning there was the Crown', since in this secular religion of the early English state the Godhead (or Crown) preceded all, established all. On 'the first day', as the barons rebelled, the Crown appeased them and included them, and the Crown created the House of Lords. On 'the second day' it created the Commons, and so on, until many days later, as the clamour from the middle classes grew, it included them too – in an expanded lower chamber. And then, as the wider public became agitated, they too were included, and the franchise for the House of Commons was extended ever further. Later, Crown as Godhead created the Church of England, the 'established Church', as an act of national assertiveness against the transnational Roman Church, which was refusing to recognise the divorce of Henry VIII. And to this day the unique relationship between Church and state (which runs against modern notions that they should be separated) allows Church of England clergy – and only them – to sit in the legislature, and establishes the Queen as the 'Supreme Governor' of the Church.

In the long history of British constitutional development, apart from the revolutionary period of the Commonwealth following the civil war, every single democratic advance, no matter how hard fought, was finally secured, not by some notion of right, but rather as an act of grace (or *noblesse oblige*) – all 'dignified' by 'royal approval'. (Indeed, and ludicrously, royal approval was even needed for Tony Benn to bring forward his Commonwealth of Britain Bill.) The key words in the British Crown's political vocabulary are 'conceded', 'gave' and 'allowed'. Of course, the heavy political reality has often seen that change is secured, not by a civilised chat, but rather by the threat of force or revolution. Even so, all the great ructions ended with the Crown intact, the 'blessing' for change delivered, and the loyalty of the people reasserted. Thus even way into the twentieth century 'the Commoners' (the elected representatives of the people) still parade into 'the Lords' to stand at the bar (the unelected peers sit) for the opening of Parliament, the Queen delivering her opening speech from – of all things – a throne.

The lowly standing given to elected persons in the ideology of English governance is emphasised by the pseudo-medieval pageantry and rituals – all royal-based and originating mainly in the nineteenth century – which surround parliamentary law-making, where the Commons gets a walk-on part: 'Be it enacted,' the sonorous tones declare, 'by the Queen's most Excellent Majesty, by and with the advice and consent of the Lords Spiritual and Temporal, and Commons, in this present Parliament assembled . . .' Thus, 'the Queen's most Excellent Majesty' remains not only the 'fount of all honour', but also the fount of political legitimacy, rather like some unseen and mystical presence set above the political fray who bestows authority on the scene, and, for a limited period, upon the political winner – as long, that is, as the winner accepts the ultimate sovereignty of the Crown.

In Britain's royal-state, the Crown is technically above the law: since the monarch *is* the state, it can hardly prosecute itself. Thus, in a theoretical sense the monarch owns the British constitution, which royal title to Britain reflects itself in the nomenclature of the Westminster routine: 'Her Majesty's Government', 'Her Majesty's Opposition' ('Loyal' of course), 'Her' Prime Minister, 'Noble Lords' and so forth. Of course, Parliament is not owned by 'Her Majesty', but in both houses the oaths, the loyal addresses, and above all the need to secure royal assent for any Bill to become an Act, all highlight the lines of authority. Most problematic, and dangerous, in Britain's royal-state, the courts are the monarch's (the reason why the monarch cannot be sued), as are the tax authorities (the reason the monarch, unlike anyone else, can choose which taxes to

24

pay) and the armed forces (whose officers take their oaths to the person of the monarch). Truly, it is a royal-state.

In theory, the royal-state may own, not only the land, but also the people on the land of 'the Kingdom'. The component parts of the modern royal-state are represented in the triptych of the Crown plus the two Houses of Parliament (hence Dicey's formulation of 'the Crown in Parliament'); this 'Crown in Parliament' is sovereign – meaning that there is no appeal against its decisions. As Dicey himself asserted, in as clear a depiction of the audacious reach of the royal-state as one can get:

> Parliament . . . has, under the English constitution, the right to make or unmake any law whatsoever; and further . . . no person or body is recognised by the law of England as having a right to override or set aside the legislation of Parliament.[4]

Dicey defined 'Parliament' as comprising the monarch, the House of Commons and the House of Lords, acting together as the 'Queen in Parliament'.

Unlike more modern polities, this royal-state is not limited by a written constitution, by a supreme court, by an entrenched system of individual rights against the state, or by a process of amendment to the constitution. Thus, theoretically at least, the royal-state has total (or totalitarian) power at its disposal. Should the 'Crown in Parliament' wish to dispose of the land of the United Kingdom or the people on it (or, for instance, declare a boy a girl), then, under the British system, it has the legal power to do so. And because the royal-state allows no supreme court or written constitution to enforce human rights, there is no higher authority – within the royal-state – to appeal to. Moreover, the royal-state's legislation can override the much-vaunted common law of England. In 1993, for example, when Princess Anne remarried, Scottish law was broken to protect her from public scrutiny. Under Scottish law any marriage must be notified fifteen days in advance, while those married previously and now remarrying need to give six weeks notice. In fact the local registrar received no notice at all. The Queen had 'enlisted'

25

the assistance of the highest judicial officer in the land, the Lord Chancellor, who advised Scotland's Registrar-General that 'no law would be broken if the notification were kept secret'.[5]

Of course, adherents of the royal-state (many of them scholars of the constitution) tend to argue that these highly theoretical nostrums are irrelevant, and that what counts is the hard practice of British government and law, where, they contend, things look much brighter and the similarities between Britain and more modern states become apparent. But the truth is that these constitutional and theoretical nostrums have been taken all too seriously over the centuries and have left their mark in the form of some of the most egregiously undemocratic features of the modern British polity, which can be traced directly back to the earlier role of monarchy, the monarchical idea, and the historic monarchical impulse to authoritative (indeed authoritarian) executive-driven rulership; they are also the product of the monarchy's continued hold on Britain's modern culture. As the *Financial Times* recently put it:

> The Crown sits at the apex of our unwritten constitution. It puts the lid on the glass jar inside which sit the suffocating elements of a Britain that should be long past: an overly-powerful executive; . . . a tradition of secrecy in the name of the Crown; a tendency for ministers to make arbitrary decisions; an obsession with maintaining the unitary structure of the United Kingdom.[6]

Take, for instance, the 'practical' use today of the 'royal prerogative' powers vested by the royal-state in the British executive. These 'royal prerogative powers' (powers that may be exercised by 'the Crown' without parliamentary authority, the source of modern Britain's overweening and obsessively secretive executive) are the direct, lineal descendant of the royal-state's arbitrary monarchical tradition. The list of these prerogatives often shocks. For instance, in the royal-state Parliament has no say over the summoning, dissolving and proroguing of itself (all that is needed is the monarch's signature); it also has no say over making treaties, declaring war, commanding the armed forces, appointing the judges, conferring honours, creating peers, appointing ministers, initiating criminal proceedings or granting pardons.[7]

In the republican constitution of the United States, the legislature at least has a say in appointing judges and cabinet ministers, and in declaring war – and, of course, its terms are fixed, so the executive branch cannot manipulate the electoral process. In royal-state Britain these impressive functions are reserved for a small group of cabinet ministers whose only limitation rests upon securing the signature of an unelected monarch.

These prerogative powers ensure that in the world of modern British politics the monarchy is still an active player. For instance, the fact that the monarch may refuse a prime minister's request for a dissolution (as was rumoured would have been the case should John Major have sought one following defeat in the 'paving Bill' for the Maastricht treaty in November 1992[8]) represents royal power over one of the most sensitive areas in any modern polity. Similarly, the Crown's formal role of appointing the prime minister, although normally routine, could, in the event of a coalition government, a hung Parliament, or simply a disagreement between the factions of a majority Party, prove highly controversial. (Of course, the formal appointment and ceremonial 'swearing in' of Britain's prime minister is conducted in secret. It has been revealed, however, that the putative prime minister has to go through a ceremony of 'kissing hands', although it is not known whether he or she is expected to kneel or merely bow.)

Harold Laski, in his criticism of the role of the King in the 1931 constitutional crisis, set out what he saw as the 'wide and pervasive' political influence of the monarch. The picture he drew then could still be painted in the 1990s:

He has the right, at the earliest possible stage, to see all the [Cabinet] papers; he must be consulted, and he can express his views. It is clear enough that a monarch who takes his duties seriously is a force to be reckoned with in our system. It is not merely that his place at the very

27

centre of affairs gives him an opportunity of continuous scrutiny and knowledge. It is not only also that what comment he may choose to make must be treated with a respect not normally accorded to the opinions of other men ... He [the Prime Minister] cannot hope to go on his way regardless of the opinions of the Crown. He must reply to its arguments, weigh its considerations, satisfy its susceptibilities in a way, and to a degree, of which the implication is clearly that if the Crown is a reserve power, it is one of which the possible exercise must never be forgotten.[9]

In fact, Britain's contemporary prime ministers have all spent inordinate amounts of time with Elizabeth II, primarily in the weekly audiences at Buckingham Palace; in any system, access to the chief executive is, in itself, a form of power.

Because royal prerogative powers are exercised by a small group of ministers in secret (needing only the sovereign's signature), the exact role of the unelected monarch over a whole range of policy must remain relatively obscure. We know that monarchs feel strongly on some issues – for instance, the present Queen has views on the role of the Commonwealth – and we also know that prime ministers are going to listen very carefully to the person to whom they swear loyalty. Also, in an unwritten constitution, powers (or functions) are very flexible instruments: they can expand and contract according to taste, and power tends to flow informally. Royal influence thrives on such informality, on behind-the-scenes fixing and on the subtle pressure exerted (particularly on some less socially confident prime ministers) by the aura of traditional authority. The ubiquitous Bagehot once divined that the function of a 'constitutional monarch' was summed up by the right to 'be informed, to encourage and to warn'. He may have understated the role.

What Bagehot (along with Dicey and Jennings and Norton *et al.*) did not address was the cultural power of the modern monarchy as it exerts itself through the royal-state apparatus. The magnitude of the appropriation by the monarchy of the

28

symbols of nationhood and authority is breath-taking. The royal head appears on the notes, coins and stamps of the subjects; members of the royal family appear at all the major national ceremonials (including remembrance events); the Queen, as head of state, is the technical commander-in-chief of Britain's armed forces; kings and queens lend their names to eras and epochs; the royal crest appears above law courts and on civil servants' briefcases; subjects in trouble are summoned by papers from the Crown Prosecution Service, and, of course, are detained 'at Her Majesty's pleasure'.

The culture of pseudo-medieval kingship bears down upon the hapless British subjects in their very daily routine. Letters are delivered by the *Royal* Mail, tax demands come in envelopes marked 'On *Her Majesty's* Service', you go to hear music at the *Royal* Albert Hall, drama at the *Royal* Shakespeare Company, opera at the *Royal* Opera, ballet at the *Royal* Ballet; you linger in the *Royal* Academy (an experience which once turned the mind of the young Hugh – now Lord – Thomas to wondering whether an 'establishment' existed), you walk in *Royal* parks and on *Crown* land, you study at *Royal* institutes and *Royal* colleges, you serve in the *Royal* Air Force and the *Royal* Navy (interestingly, not yet in the *Royal* Army), you eat, drink and use goods made by *Royal* Appointment, you can live in or visit people in *Royal* boroughs in streets called *Queen's* Terrace or *King's* Row or *Princes* Street. You can win the *Queen's* award. So intrusive is the highly personalised culture of royalty that even the English National Ballet's van parades 'Patron: HRH The Princess of Wales' on its side.

The transmission of the images and values of monarchy into the present day is secured not only by the institutions of Whitehall and Westminster but also by the subtle, and not so subtle, royal involvement in the nooks and crannies of British public life. For instance, the Church of England, the 'official Church', boasts the Queen as its 'Supreme Governor'. The media, particularly the state-funded 'official media', the BBC, still persist with the royal-state's 'national' anthem at the end of broadcasting, still portray the royal family in reverential terms, and even still produce artificial sickly smiles on the news whenever a royal event is broadcast. Most universities still boast some royal patron who hands out the prizes at the degree-awarding ceremony. Even the great sporting events kick off with the anthem 'God Save our Gracious Queen'.

The cultural reach of this one institution (and one family) over a whole country has no parallel in the Western world. In terms of its command over media space and time, public events and imagery and everyday words, the British monarchy must rank alongside the Communist Party of the Soviet Union at the height of its power. How, and to what extent, this cultural domination counts must remain something of a mystery. That monarchy has helped determine the system of government (what I describe as the royal-state) is obvious. That there is some relationship between the values of monarchy and the political and social culture of modern Britain seems highly probable. Arguably, Britain's political tradition of paternalism, and the allegiant culture that goes with it, may be a direct product of the royal patrimony. Whether there is a corresponding connection between the values of monarchy and economic performance is more problematic. But even though it cannot be measured, the issue can hardly be dismissed.

How is one to explain the astonishing fact that, for most of the post-war period, hardly any criticism of the royal family or the system of monarchy appeared in any mass-circulation outlet? How could the (by present standards) timid critique of the Queen by John Grigg and Malcolm Muggeridge in the post-war period provoke such a hostile reaction that both men, for a time, were treated as notorious outcasts? How did the monarchy manage to sail on, untouched and secure, through the early 1960s' burst of political satire, when even the radical humour of the television programme *That Was The Week That Was*, aimed directly at landed grandee incompetence and upper-class stupidity, did not attack them?

In the whole post-war period from 1945 up until the late 1980s, no serious republican book was published.[10] Why not? Why until the late 1980s did not a single republican article (in the sense of a systematic critique of monarchy and an open advocacy of its replacement) appear in any major national newspaper? Why until the late 1980s was hardly any television coverage critical of the monarchy, or advocating a republic, aired in democratic and open-minded Britain?

If the cultural reach of the monarchy until recently succeeded in keeping the lid so firmly in place on criticism of its own position – if its instincts for self-preservation succeeded so effectively in shaping the political response to itself – is it not right to conclude that the monarchy, so far from the impotence which its protectors claim for it, has, through the culture it has spawned, demonstrated a highly effective ability to exercise political power?

From the sublime to the ridiculous

Publicly expressed attitudes towards monarchy – if not to the wider apparatus of the royal-state – have passed through a series of phases. For most of the post-war period – from Elizabeth Windsor's accession to the throne in 1952 until well into the 1980s – the monarchy was impregnable. (The surname 'Windsor' was adopted in 1917 during the First World War in order to deflect anti-German sentiment. It was suggested by Lord Stamfordham after he discovered that Edward III was called 'Edward of Windsor'.) Critiques of the institution were few and far between, and criticism of the persons isolated and trivial, overwhelmed by a seemingly widespread (and seemingly almost total) public affection that often bordered on the adulatory. In the early 1960s Charles Petrie could write: 'For the first few years of her reign the Queen was the subject of an adulation unparalleled since the days of Louis XIV, and calculated to turn much older heads than hers.'[11] This adulation continued for much longer than the first few years of the reign, and heads were still turning well into the 1960s. This piece of writing was not in any sense unusual: 'I saw the Queen at Ascot wearing a simple coat. She gave me a smile I will never forget. I burst into tears as she reached my heart. How many women will you find like her? One in a million.'[12]

Later, in the 1970s and 1980s, comment on royalty was less fulsome, but it remained reverential. Typical of the post-war consensus was the view from the writer Andrew Duncan that 'the Queen's greatest contribution could be as a focus for civilised living';[13] or, from a cabinet minister, William Waldegrave, that 'the Royal Family is respected more than the peers ... and more than members of the House of Commons';[14] or, from the then MP Norman St John Stevas (now Lord St John of Fawsley), that 'the example of a united family life set by the Queen and her consort is a real contribution to the nation's morality'.[15] All the time, as we have seen, the institution itself was rarely subject to analysis, let alone criticism.

With this kind of public reception in a global environment in which monarchy was widely seen as anachronistic, and where outside Britain it had survived only by coming to terms with the modern world and by cutting out the pomp and slimming itself down, the House of Windsor had clearly done very well for itself. Yet the Windsors had survived and prospered well into the post-war period for reasons that are somewhat unedifying – for they had saved themselves by taking advantage of the unpleasant mix of circumstances that hit post-war Britain and lasted well into the 1980s.

The country came out of the Second World War deeply unsure of itself and its place in the world. Instead of facing up to the new circumstances – as the French and the Germans were forced to – a grey, depressed and near-defeated Britain found an escape in the institutionalised, indeed constitutionalised, fantasy land of the House of Windsor. On the one hand, the Windsors, led by the 'young Elizabeth' in the new 'Elizabethan age', turned themselves into an 'ideal' and idealised family; on the other hand, the royals, through the royal-state, provided big-time pomp for a nation which, though economically weak, and dependent upon a super-power an ocean away for its security in the Cold War, was still clinging to the self-deluding culture of Empire.

In this environment none of Britain's post-war governments was even going to raise the possibility of tackling the monarchy or reforming the royal-state. Labour's radicalism under Attlee, though high on the rhetoric of reform based upon socialist principles of equality, did not stretch to questioning the role of the monarchy. Apart from the occasional egalitarian gesture – such as Ernest Bevin's decision when Foreign Secretary to turn up at a Buckingham Palace function in his lounge suit – the new left-wing government took the lead in ushering in an era in which monarchy sat easily (perhaps appropriately) atop a paternalist welfare state. And after its victory in the 1951 election, the Conservative Party, which, after all, remained the historic party of King and court, could hardly be expected to reform what was shaping up as a monarchy with popular support.

During the 1964 election Harold Wilson campaigned for his 'New Britain' on the theme of social modernisation. Stuffy manners and ancient hierarchies were subject to ridicule, and Wilson attacked the 'gentlemen and players society' as well as the Prime Minister, Sir Alec Douglas-Home – as a 'fourteenth Earl'. Wilson himself (a meritocrat from the North of England who paraded in a classless Gannex raincoat) represented the hopes of those who sought a more modern nation that would finally put to rest Britain's ancient social forms and values. Yet this meritocratic zeal did not translate itself into action – certainly not against the royal-state or the monarchy. When Wilson's friend Richard Crossman, who became the royal-state's 'Lord President of the Council', failed in his attempt to reform the House of Lords by abolishing the hereditary element, there was absolutely no attempt by this Labour government to widen the debate they had opened up about the House of Lords to include the monarchy. No suggestion, not even a whisper, emerged about modernising and updating it. Wilson continued the tradition of Labour as a key pillar of the royal-state.

The man who replaced Wilson as prime minister after the 1970 election, Edward Heath, was also a meritocrat. His instincts were not those of the traditional royal-state Tory: he was the first Tory leader since the war who had nothing of the patrician in him; and, remarkable as it may now seem, he was the first ever to be elected! Unlike Wilson, Heath backed up his modernising impulse by a reform of one of the most sensitive aspects of the royal-state: he refused to create any new hereditary peerages. Yet even Heath, whose passions ran counter to the culture of the royal-state, possessed little energy for addressing the issue of modernising the monarchy, let alone abolishing it.

Of course, all governments since the mid-1960s were overwhelmed by economic woes, and — seemingly certain that there was no relationship between Britain's antique institutions, a backward culture and economic performance — they avoided constitutional reform. So, too, did Margaret Thatcher's three Conservative administrations, whose radical zeal was spent in trying to create an enterprise economy. Thatcherite Tories certainly saw some connection between economics and culture — hence the rhetoric about the need for an 'enterprise culture' — but Thatcher herself went against the meritocratic grain she so often professed, by restoring the hereditary peerage when she created a title for the Tory grandee, William Whitelaw.

So long as the Queen and the monarchy remained popular, no politician of the post-war era, no matter how good the case, was even going to mention the institution, except in terms of the utmost reverence. Even as late as the early 1990s, when the monarchy was becoming distinctly frayed around the edges, the political class was cautious about opening up the issue. The public in general may have become less supportive of the monarchy, but there remained a sizeable group of older people — particularly women — who identified with the Queen, and whose support politicians could not afford to lose. Thus it was only the state of the marriages of two of the Queen's sons that enabled the taboo finally to be broken.

Royal romance reached its apogee in 1981, with the wedding of Prince Charles to a 19-year-old virgin, Diana Spencer ('the love match of the century' as one tabloid newspaper dubbed it); following this, the mythology began to unravel. First to go was Anne, whose marriage to Mark Phillips ended in divorce. The experiment with commoners failed as, one by one, members of the royal family were unable to adapt to democratic union. More spectacular than Anne and Mark was the public collapse of the marriage of the Duke and Duchess of York. While the establishment succeeded in convincing a still complaisant British public that 'Fergie' was in some way unsuited to royal life, this strategy ran into an insuperable obstacle when, as it became clear that the marriage of the heir to the throne was also in trouble, the same tactics were tried with Diana. She remained popular; and whatever residual support Charles Windsor could muster dissolved when it was revealed that the heir to the throne – and the Supreme Governor-elect of the Church of England – was openly and spectacularly unfaithful to his wife.

The institution of monarchy – that most sacred of the royal-state's apartments – was now invaded; from a royalist perspective it must have been a raw experience, as if the public had suddenly arrived in charabancs, had been let inside and were sizing up the place – and were not particularly keen on what they saw. The result was a mass of critical comment in the first months of 1992. In *The Times*, columnist Janet Daley, under the robust headline 'AN ENEMY OF THE PEOPLE', called for an end to the 'dangerous fixation with the royal family',[16] while Brian Appleyard produced a longish and serious article on the dubious future of the institution.[17] The *Daily Telegraph* declared in its series 'A Family Under The Microscope' that 'The British Monarchy is today under greater pressure and stress than for many years', and that 'criticisms of the Royal family's cost, lifestyle and relevance have never been sharper'.[18] 'WHY ROYALTY HAS HAD ITS DAY', wrote A. N. Wilson in the *London Evening Standard*.[19] The *Sunday Times*, which had led the journalistic way in developing a serious critique of the monarchy, opened 1992 with an article by Robert Harris headlined 'QUEEN IN A TARNISHED CROWN MUST PUT HER HOUSE IN ORDER', in which he argued that 'the monarchy is in a mess and its woes will worsen';[20] this was followed up by serialisations of Phillip Hall's critique of royal finances, *Royal Fortune*,[21] and Andrew Morton's revelations about the private life of the Princess of Wales.[22] The *Guardian*, on its education pages, presented both the case for and, unprecedentedly, the case against monarchy, arguing that 'both monarchists and republicans have strong arguments to back up their case for tradition or change in Britain'.[23] No wonder the commentator Ludovic Kennedy – who himself publicly expressed the hope that the 'collective public life of today's royal family ... was moving peacefully towards its close' – could declare that in the early months of 1992 'the monarchy has taken a drubbing such as I have not seen in my lifetime'.[24]

By the end of the fateful year of 1992 – following a spectacular fire at Windsor Castle and a too hasty government announcement that the tax-payer alone would foot the repair bill – the flood of public criticism which engulfed the Queen slipped over, for the very first time since the turn of the century, into serious public discussion of republicanism. Even the pro-monarchist *Daily Mail* asserted, darkly, that 'by misinterpreting the present mood the Queen and her Ministers risk far more than they may realise'.[25] And in a radical commentary that captured the mood of many middle-class professionals, Joe Rogaly in the *Financial Times* argued that 'what is really needed is the dis-establishment of the monarchy'.[26]

The criticism of the monarchy which followed the great fire of Windsor took its toll on royal tradition and etiquette. There were no public opinion polls published in the immediate aftermath of the fire, but a very random sample of callers to an LBC radio programme revealed a surprisingly large majority hostile to the monarchy and the role of the Queen.[27] In a speech in the Guildhall in London in late November the Queen herself entered the fray with an unprecedented defence of her role. She described the year 1992 as *'annus horribilis'*, and, surprisingly, publicly criticised her critics. The tone was defensive, and her call for public sympathy, set against the splendour and pomp of her backdrop, let alone her life and lifestyle in the midst of a recession, seemed faintly absurd.

The Guildhall speech was followed by the government's announcement that the Queen had, after all, decided to break with recent tradition and pay some taxes. 'The amount she will pay – expected to be about £2 million a year – is relatively small', declared a daily newspaper, 'but [may be] seen as a symbolic gesture to spare the Royal Family from further attacks.'[28] Whether such an obviously political move by Buckingham Palace – a 'voluntary' offer, the details of which remained obscure, but which certainly did not include inheritance tax

– would indeed spare the royal family further attacks remained unclear. The problem for the monarchy was that, once the principle of tax-paying had been conceded by the Queen (I use the term conceded because the decision of the Queen to pay some tax was a 'voluntary' one, strangely not determined or demanded by the elected government), they possessed little in the way of an intellectual defence against being treated like anyone else on the tax question. It could only be a matter of time before the full 'Royal Fortune' was subject to serious scrutiny.

The speech and the tax concession could not, ultimately, serve to remove the monarchy and royal family from the spotlight of criticism and analysis. The problem was that although, by having yielded to public pressure to change, the monarchy revealed itself as less than magical, less than mysterious, and subject to the same pressures as anyone else, at the same time it continued to rely upon mystique and distinctiveness to remain, in certain important constitutional senses, above the law. This was a serious dichotomy that could not be sustained for too long.

As controversy continued over the next few days, more and more public figures began declaring themselves dissatisfied with the monarchy, among them many who for the first time were reported as embracing republicanism. Among them were such public and establishment figures as Christopher Price, director of Leeds Metropolitan University; Anthony Scrivener, a QC and former chairman of the Bar; Ludovic Kennedy; Claire Rayner; and the novelist Sue Townsend.[29] However, the vast majority of those commenting in the newspapers and on the television, particularly politicians who had taken oaths to the Queen, or journalists whose livelihood depended upon the continuance of the monarchy, remained critical but were careful not to stray beyond a 'reformist' stance.

There was a distinct lack, in the public commentary at the height of the monarchy's November 1992 mini-crisis, of any systematic or theoretical opposition to what is, after all, the essence of monarchy – the vital principle of constitutional heredity. Instead – and this is a telling point about contemporary British values – most of the royal critics were, understandably in a recession, primarily concerned about the practical matter of money. Hard cash was at the root of the damage suffered by the royal reputation following the Windsor fire. The castle was going to be rebuilt at public expense, and the weakest point in the monarchy's general line of defence was its tax status. At the height of the controversy, although the *Guardian*'s Alex Brummer produced the most detailed newspaper explanation of royal finances yet to appear, it went unaccompanied by any analysis of the institution of monarchy or its republican alternative.[30]

Opinion polls were also reflecting a changing public mood towards Britain's royals. A poll by Market Opinion Research International (MORI) carried out for the *Sunday Times* in June 1992 showed that only one in two Britons believed that 'the nation would be worse off if the monarchy was abolished' (down from 63 per cent in 1987 and 77 per cent in 1984). Thirty-four per cent thought abolition would make no difference. Most damaging of all to the royal-state was the public's view that the monarchy was an institution linked to the past, with serious intimations of mortality: although 84 per cent believed the monarchy would still be around in 2002, only 46 per cent believed it would still be with us in fifty years' time, and only 29 per cent believed the institution would survive another century.[31] At around the same time an *Observer*/Harris poll revealed that 76 per cent of those polled thought the Queen should pay tax, and that support for the outright abolition of the monarchy had more than doubled – from the low base of 6 per cent in 1990 to 15 per cent in 1992.[32]

An even more devastating poll appeared after the announcement of the separation of the Prince and Princess of Wales. 'For the first time in recent years, a clear majority thinks Britain would be at least as well off if we axed the monarchy,' suggested the *Sunday Times*'s correspondents in reporting the MORI poll carried out for the *Sunday Times* and published on 13 December 1992, which revealed that 37 per cent of those polled thought Britain would be worse off if 'we abolished the monarchy', 17 per cent thought 'we would be better off', and

42 per cent thought 'it would make no difference', a figure up 13 per cent from the preceding poll.

Support for the monarchy was also slipping away in the more cautious political world. In a poll of MPs published by the *Sunday Telegraph* on 24 January 1993, again in the backwash of the news of the royal separation, 14 per cent of Labour MPs questioned favoured no change, while 32 per cent favoured reforming the monarchy and a full 24 per cent favoured a republic. This news from the Labour Party front would have been received in Buckingham Palace with much more consternation than mere shifts in public opinion: the monarchy, in order to survive, needs a bi-partisan political climate to support it.

There were many other straws in the wind. For instance, in an area where actions, not words (or responses to questions), count, it was revealed that there had been a steep decline in viewing figures for one of the royal-state's most 'traditional' of institutions – the Queen's Christmas Broadcast (down from 17 million in the early 1980s to 10 million in 1991).[33]

Whatever happened to the reverence?

What had happened to the reverence? Why had light been let in on Bagehot's 'magic'? And why had it happened during the early 1990s, and so quickly? As with most sudden changes of public mood among opinion-formers, the answer probably lies in a conjunction of events. Of course, the highly publicised personal problems of the younger royals, and the dogged refusal of the Queen to pay taxes, did not help the House of Windsor's public relations image. Yet unedifying personal behaviour among royals is nothing new; and increasing public disquiet about these marginal issues does not, in itself, say anything in particular about the validity (or otherwise) of the institution of monarchy. What did make a difference was the coincidence of the personal shortcomings of the royals with the culmination of profound post-war social changes on the one hand, and, on the other, a public perception that Britain was on the verge (particularly in its relationship with an integrating Europe) of a new political era. The standard royal revelations and problems acted as a trigger to assess how the institution of monarchy fitted in with these changes.

Among the most important of these social changes is the sad (for monarchists) fact that the British are simply less deferential than they used to be. Magic no longer rules. As Bagehot himself argued, 'reverence for royalty could not doubtless continue among a cultivated population, a population capable of abstract ideas; it would not be required'.[34] The British are now less in awe both of the traditional 'upper classes' and of a whole range of traditional institutions. 'During the 1980s,' wrote James Buchan, 'something occurred to estrange the public from the glamorous features of British constitutional life, which seemed to lose any structural purpose and became mere decoration: quaint, folkloric, a little tiresome.'[35] In other words, with an ever increasing distance between the memory of the old Empire and the pressures of the Thatcherite version of economic realism, the 1980s saw the British begin to lose their social pretensions (and illusions); they were becoming more like the Americans.

The raw affirmation of tradition, the assertion that because 'it's always been there' it possesses some kind of intrinsic worth, is no longer sufficient argument. In Britain, as throughout the West, 'tradition' is falling both to reason and to consumerism. Increasingly, even in England, people want to know the rationale for institutions (particularly those they fund with their tax money and are supposed to owe loyalty to). And increasingly, too, questions about 'value for money' are the order of the day – a test which automatically makes the monarchy more dependent upon the market and the people, and thus more vulnerable. (Indeed, a poll in the summer of 1992 showed that 60 per cent of voters under 25 possessed little affection for the royal family and believed that the country did not 'get value for money' from them.)[36]

The idea that every institution should be judged by its merits, no longer simply by the fact of its existence, by its lineage or longevity, was arguably one of the most useful features of the market ideology of the 1980s; and its continuing vitality is potentially devastating not only for the monarchy but for all the institutions of the *ancien régime* royal-state. Once released from the spell of history and acceptance, some very basic questions are likely to be asked. Why should a person be head of state, or sit in the legislature and exercise political power, simply because of the accident of birth? Why should the monarch be above the law and not be subject to all taxes, including inheritance tax? Why should an institution's survival be so dependent upon deference? These questions have an insistent ring about them; once asked, they will not go away.

Looking to the future, there is little that can be done to immunise the monarchy from this new approach. The popular newspaper columnist Nigel Dempster believes that the monarchy is doomed because, over time, it will not be able to justify itself to an increasingly sceptical electorate. Referring to the royal family he has argued: 'They're in an increasingly cleft stick . . . when the Queen dies . . . there would have been a decade or so of unrest at the role of the monarchy . . . I can see a Parliament of the future holding a referendum and the vote going against the monarchy.'[37] Indeed, even in the absence of such a vote the simple growth of republican sentiment places the monarchy in trouble. Its 'neutrality', its sense of 'being above' the political battle, is crucial to its health. Gladstone understood this point all too well when he advised Queen Victoria to return to public life in 1871, using the Thanksgiving Service for the Prince of Wales's recovery as a vehicle. But whereas the Victorian monarchy came out fighting in the 1870s, that of Elizabeth Windsor has resorted to a rearguard action. Its gravamen has been to make the institution more relevant and open, more interesting to a younger audience: to introduce it on the one hand as 'engaged' in modern issues and on the other as a modern, somewhat idealised, family. Professor James Curran has argued that this new tack has 'back-fired . . . Increasing accessibility has led to increasing criticism.'[38] What is more, the attempt to engage in contemporary 'issues' (a speciality of Prince Charles) has naturally led to controversy and to the alienation of some important leaders of public opinion. Most damaging of all was the strategy of presenting the monarchy as an institutionalised and symbolic ideal (and idealised) family. This particular piece of image-making was always a high-risk strategy, for the royal actors concerned needed to aim beyond 'normal' standards of behaviour to moral norms that the public still aspired to achieve. When a mass-circulation newspaper editor could write that the 'devastating evidence of affairs by both the Duchess of York and the Prince of Wales ... were knock-out blows to the royals' carefully nurtured public image of the exemplary British family, a closely knit unit protecting the values that we all hold dear', there was little that royal supporters could say in reply.[39] The combination of dwindling public deference and a continuing popular sense of moral rectitude proved a combustible mix.

Unfortunately for the monarchy, changing social attitudes at home happened to coincide with dramatic political changes affecting Britain's position in the world. The first of these was the end of Empire. The British monarchy had been reinvented under Victoria (and her public-relations-conscious husband) to represent and reflect the exalted place of Britain as a conquering nation managing a worldwide imperial system. Victoria was 'Empress of India', among other high-sounding titles; crucially for the development of the transnational monarchy, she was also the head of state of the nations of the far-flung colonial system. The monarchy became the symbol of imperial unity and the constitutional link between the metropolitan homeland and the imperial possessions. At Queen Victoria's diamond jubilee in 1897, at Edward VII's coronation in 1902, George V's in 1911 and George VI's in 1937, contingents from the nations of the Empire marched through the streets of London to honour their 'sovereign'.

Of course, the demise of the Empire (a relatively swift affair which took place over about a decade and a half between 1945 and the late 1960s) placed the monarchy in an awkward position. As de-colonisation gathered pace during the reign of Elizabeth II, the decision was taken to straddle the monarchy between the island home on the one hand and the emerging independent nations on the other. A 'Commonwealth of Nations' was created, and the British monarch became head of state of both: 'Head of the Commonwealth' as well as British 'sovereign'. This in fact extended the reach of the royal-state, which took on a supra-national role, as not only the monarch but also the House of Lords, the Privy Council and the judiciary possessed varying degrees of jurisdiction outside the domestic realm, and over the peoples of Australia, New Zealand, Canada and other nations.

This unwieldy edifice was not without its tensions, and sections of Tory opinion remained sceptical about whether a transnational monarchy could properly serve the interests of the British state and people.[40] Yet the 'Commonwealth of Nations' was established to do just that: to act as a crutch for British pride during major changes in its world role. Arnold Smith, who was Commonwealth General-Secretary from 1965 to 1975, made this point when he suggested that to make a change 'would deeply upset British opinion at a time when Britain is still going through the neurosis of diminished relative power in the world'.[41] The Queen, however, took her new role all too seriously. She felt her special contribution to the modern monarchy would be precisely to emphasise her role as Head of the Commonwealth. But ironically, the Commonwealth role – while helpful as a transitional arrangement both for people and for royal-state – also exposed the monarchy to the republican sentiment that has grown in many parts of the rickety transnational royal-state system, particularly in Canada and Australia. Should some Commonwealth countries eventually decide either to leave the Commonwealth or to remove the Queen as head of their own states, her diminished role abroad would leave her with little more global status than that possessed by the queens of Holland or Denmark.

Increasingly, the British monarchy will have to fall back on its final redoubt: the British nation-state, to which its future is linked and where its fate will be determined. Yet as we have seen, the news from the home front does not bode well for the monarchy: at the very moment when the monarchy needs for its survival a nation-state based upon national sovereignty, the nature of that national sovereignty is increasingly being questioned.

There can be little doubt that its association with the nation-state is at the very heart of the monarchy's legitimacy in British life. The monarch is 'head' of this British 'sovereign state', represents this 'sovereign state', and through the strange notion of 'Crown' defines the jurisdiction and territory of the 'sovereign state'. Also, the political idea of 'national sovereignty' – so much a feature of the British debate about Europe – is bound up with the notion of the 'sovereign' – not because the idea of 'national sovereignty' is dependent upon a Queen, but rather because for many Britons the Queen still expresses the idea of 'national sovereignty'.

The reality of a British 'sovereign state' – inviolate, deter-mining its own future regardless of outside forces – is an anachronism in a new world based upon plural (as opposed to 'sovereign') realities, upon global markets and the economic and political bloc of Europe. Even so, it was this issue that continued to mesmerise the British as late as the 1980s and 1990s. This was the reason for the emollient term (serving the same function as the 'Commonwealth of Nations') 'pooling sovereignties' – which emerged primarily through the speeches of the pro-European Foreign Secretary, Sir Geoffrey Howe – to describe Britain's loss of independence in an increasingly integrated Europe. Yet, of course, like virginity, 'sovereignty' is an absolutist concept: you either possess it or you don't. The fact was that Britain had lost it, and formally so. And with it went yet another nail in the royal-state's coffin.

3·The Cost of the Royal-state

T he monarchy has added little to the development of Britain as a serious country. In fact the opposite is the case: it was not by its kings and queens that England defined itself, but rather by clipping the wings of monarchy and then, later, by overthrowing monarchical despotism and the 'divine right of kings'. After the union, the development of Britain – the industrial and scientific revolution, the extension of the franchise, the emergence of the country as one of the most prosperous and powerful nations in the world – owed little or nothing to the fact that it possessed kings and queens. The monarchy, lucky to have survived, was a beneficiary, not a cause, of the ascent of Britain during the age of commerce and reform.

It was probably inevitable that with the decline of the country in the twentieth century the monarchy should become so prominent a feature of the nation's life. Yet it is during this century, when the country has desperately needed to adapt to its changed circumstances, that the monarchy and its royal-state has taken its toll. The political, social and cultural costs – in attitudes and values – cannot be measured, but is huge. The financial cost of the royal-state, however, can be counted.

The top apparatus of Britain's royal-state is overblown. As well as the extended royal family itself there is a Royal Household including administrators, clerks, footmen, housemaids, chefs, chauffeurs and, of course, the more elevated titles like Master of

45

the Household, Keeper of the Privy Purse, Crown Equerry and so forth.[1] In 1983, the Royal Household alone numbered 323 or more persons (about the size of the teaching staff of a new university).[2] There is also a peculiar and somewhat mysterious body called the Privy Council which, although outside Parliament and not responsible to it, retains a staff of its own and still has various important functions. It is presided over by the Queen and a cabinet minister called the Lord President of the Council. And, of course, there is also the House of Lords which although unelected remains one of the largest legislatures in the Western world. Hereditary and life peers together make up well over 1300 eligible law-makers.

However, the financial cost of this royal court network is not particularly scandalous if measured as a percentage of Gross Domestic Product. Indeed, any serious, commercially minded manager of a Ruritanian tourist theme-park might even consider it 'value for money'. However, the expenditure is excessive by comparison with the typical costs involved in keeping other heads of state – including the President of the United States.[3] The American President, who has a serious job to do on top of his ceremonial functions, has available to him, courtesy of the tax-payer, only the relatively small living accommodations of the White House family quarters, and the equally unpretentious living areas of Camp David in the Maryland hills. There is now no longer a presidential yacht, nor a presidential train. By comparison, Britain's publicly funded royal homes make up an impressive array of royal palaces and other residences – Windsor, Buckingham Palace, St James's Palace, Clarence House, Kensington Palace, Marlborough House, Hampton Court and Holyroodhouse in Edinburgh. The Queen also has her private castles at Sandringham and Balmoral.

Philip Hall, in his revealing account of royal wealth, states that the royals are 'often said to be inexpensive':

yet the figure [around £5 million, borne by the tax-payer, a figure suggested by royal *sympathisers*] is only the tip of the iceberg. Once the costs, borne by the government, of running the Royal Yacht, *Britannia*, the Royal Train, aircraft, palaces and so on are included the total rises to more than £50 million per annum.[4]

This sum amounts to the cost per year of two new universities.

What is scandalous – by comparison with the standards set by the more advanced political systems – is the constitutional position of royal wealth. Like the Queen herself, royal money and royal wealth are above the law, with the Queen in the pleasant position of being the only Briton able to determine her financial affairs (both her income from the state and her liabilities) by secret negotiations with the Prime Minister. By contrast, the American President can expect, not only to pay tax in exactly the same way as any other US citizen, but to see a photograph of his tax return displayed for all to see on the pages of mass-circulation newspapers. Any whisper that he might not be being treated equally with everyone else could lead to an immediate congressional investigation, if not to impeachment.

By comparison, the taxes paid by the British head of state (a person far richer than the American, French, German and other European presidents combined), in a system enacted most recently during the 1992 November mini-crisis, amount to a kind of voluntary 'donation' to the Exchequer, one not set by law and not even solicited by the government. The Queen's finances are also treated differently (from those of the public, and from those of many foreign heads of state) in the matter of share-holdings. The contemporary demand for 'transparency' in government is decidedly under-employed by the obviously obfuscatory system – using a body called 'The Bank of England Nominees' – which is specifically designed to hide from public view royal family holdings of shares.[5]

The Royal Household, like the sovereign, can exempt itself from laws which apply to all other subjects. The monarch's household often lobbies the government in order to achieve these exemptions, and on other occasions it uses the arcane notion of Crown immunity to escape implementing the law. For instance, the Royal Household is not obligated to enforce the Race Relations Act. The Queen, or her agent, could therefore act quite legally in refusing to employ a West Indian cleaning

47

woman on the grounds that she was black. Phillip Hall has suggested that 'this immunity, perhaps, is needed to save the Queen, as head of the multi-racial Commonwealth and a multi-racial Britain, from infringing the Trade Descriptions Act'.[6]

There is also a problem in the twilight world that exists between what is public and what is private. The royal art collections are, in essence, one of the 'inalienable' properties of the Crown – that is, they pass automatically into the ownership and control of whoever is sovereign. But what does the concept of 'inalienability' really mean? Does it make the collections – say the one at Windsor Castle – public property? Well, not quite, for they are privately administered. Or again, is it appropriate that a public figure as important as the head of state should derive profits from vast tracts of privately owned land in her own country – title to which land (the Duchy of Lancaster) remains obscure and controversial?[7]

The sad fact is that the royal family and Royal Household could easily have secured from the public purse adequate, even lavish, resources, while at the same time agreeing to abide by modern notions of openness, accountability and equality of treatment under the law. Yet at no point, not even in an age in which openness and democratic accountability have virtually been constitutional standards, has the monarchy offered, or the government insisted, that such a step be taken. (Offering to pay *some* taxes of your choice is not the same as agreeing to abide by the laws governing all other persons.)

The system of handling the royal finances amounts to little less than a statement to the nation: that in the highest reaches of the royal-state the idea of equality before the law – one of the bedrock principles of Western democratic development – is not valued. Such a declamation is, though, well within keeping with its broader ideology of governance.

The cost that cannot be counted

The above are all costs that can be counted; what cannot be measured in pounds and pennies or in the extravagant apparatus of the royal-state is the damage that the monarchical idea has done to British society and culture over centuries – and particularly during the more recent industrial and commercial era when Britain needed to democratise and modernise its economy and society in order to compete in an increasingly global marketplace.

It is a genuinely difficult task to establish any relationship between social and political values on the one hand, and economic performance on the other. However, it would seem that, other things being equal, those countries which value commerce, industry, science, enterprise, equal opportunity and social mobility are more likely to succeed economically than those which place a value upon, say, country life, high art, tradition, inherited privilege and social hierarchy. Britain, of course, pioneered the industrial society, but the triumph of commercial values was never complete. Instead, the Victorian liberal dream of a classless, capitalist society foundered upon a harder, primarily English, reality: the desire among the new industrialists to ape their 'betters' on the land. As a former Education Secretary, Sir Keith Joseph, has argued:

> Britain never internalised capitalist values ... On the contrary the rich man sought to get away from his background in trade and industry, giving his son not an education in capitalist values but against them, in favour of the older values of army, church, upper civil service, professions and land owning.[8]

Martin Weiner's slim volume, *English Culture and the Decline of the Industrial Spirit* (1987), is still the most authoritative account of how nineteenth-century Britain resisted modernity. He has argued that what we witnessed then was nothing less than a rejection of industrialism by the leaders of Victorian society (what today we would call the 'opinion-formers'): 'I became aware of a distinctive complex of social ideas, sentiments and values in the articulate classes embodying an ambiguous attitude towards modern industrial society.' Having started mankind on 'the great ascent', Britain, Weiner

49

suggests, took 'the wrong path', and 'economic growth was frequently viewed with suspicion and disdain'.[9] Indeed, the cultural and intellectual climate was not only disdainful towards commerce, but actively hostile, even to the point of seeing the emergence of a business culture as threatening the moral balance of society. In this reactionary climate high Tories and socialists could make common cause. Lord Robert Cecil would have had considerable support from the upper-middle-class Fabians when he denounced the Chamberlain business family as being 'sordid and materialistic . . . on the high road to corruption'.[10]

The 'great ascent' in Britain took place within a feudal template – that is, within a political system in which monarchy and aristocracy, although yielding to mass democratic demands, nonetheless retained their formal constitutional symbolism and social power. Thus, as Richard Cobden exasperatedly observed of early-nineteenth-century capitalists:

> We have the spirit of feudalism rife and rampant in the midst of the antagonistic development of the age of Watt, Arkwright and Stephenson! Nay, feudalism is every day more in the ascendant in political and social life. So great is its power and prestige that it draws to it the support and homage of even those who are the natural leaders of the newer and better civilisation. Manufacturers and merchants as a rule seem only to desire riches that they may be enabled to prostrate themselves at the feet of feudalism. How is this to end?[11]

For these Victorian industrialists the ultimate accolade was not the money made or the capital accumulated, nor even what could be bought or learnt or created with commerce's riches. Rather, the ultimate satisfaction would be social acceptance – a peerage, a place at court and a country estate – the full immersion in the very feudalism their industrial prowess had supposedly helped to destroy.

It certainly remains an arguable proposition that the continued existence of monarchy – both as a political reality

50

and as a social symbol – ensured that for the upwardly mobile nineteenth-century Briton, cultural and social power still lay outside the marketplace; and that as a consequence the 'great ascent' left us, certainly by comparison with other Western nations, if not on the foothills, then certainly not at the summit. Had the supporters of 'The Good Old Cause' in the seventeenth century properly completed their revolution, and had the Commonwealth matured into a normal bourgeois republic, then, at the very least, the political and social template within which the later industrial revolution took place would have allowed commercial (and associated liberal) values to develop more freely and naturally.

Alongside the rejection of industrial and commercial values went a predominant cultural disdain for science, technology and for modernity itself. Robert Adams has argued:

> In the late nineteenth century, a few practical steps to stimulate technical innovation would not have been beyond Britain's capacity [but] by contrast with the German universities, Oxford and Cambridge displayed a disinterest in science for which provincial and Scottish schools only partially atoned.[12]

Correlli Barnett, writing before Weiner, has offered a similar critique. His major work, *The Collapse of British Power* (1972), located some of the origins of Britain's other-worldly, anti-commercial and anti-modern culture in the character of education delivered by the mid-Victorian public schools, a standard set by the pioneering influence of Dr Thomas Arnold, headmaster of Rugby School from 1827 until his death in 1841. Barnett argues that under Arnold's influence a crucial social dimension was added to intellectual development. In the syllabuses of these schools a remote academicism – in which science and other modern subjects were distrusted – emerged as part of a more 'general education for life'. Barnett argues that this 'education for life' was unconducive to both intellectual enquiry and commercial realism. He argues that 'the qualities imparted to this future ruling class by their education – probity, orthodoxy, romantic idealism,

51

a strong sense of public responsibility – admirably fitted them for running the British Empire as they saw it'.[13]

The rejection of industrial values in favour of a patrician code of governance often took the form of a militant aestheticism – an approach decried by Herbert Spencer. In its concern for elegance, it forgot substance. Intellectual attributes – knowledge, data and hard analysis – were less valued than social refinement, polish and éclat. 'Teaching the graces', in which behaviour becomes all, was thus a reaction against the perceived terrors of Victorian commerce.

By the turn of the nineteenth century it could certainly be argued that the governing impulses of a network of British educators – running from the public schools through to Oxbridge – were as much social as academic. The British still seemed to regard the chief function of the universities as producing rounded 'young gentlemen' – a feature of academic life which the British educationalist A. H. Halsey suggests has continued right up to the present mass-higher-education era.[14]

Thus, during the all-important nineteenth century (when in other Western countries capitalism and democratisation were triumphant), the British retained an almost feudal, pre-modern obsession with non-industrial landed values. This Victorian 'revolt' against business and industry, science and modernity took place within a society which still boasted a socially powerful monarchy and aristocracy, and whose political structures (primarily the House of Lords) were still redolent of the institutions of feudalism. Whether 'the revolt' helped perpetuate the legitimacy of feudal institutions (including the monarchy), or, alternatively, whether feudal institutions and values induced 'the revolt', remains a difficult question. What is certain is that, because of this peculiar pattern of cultural development in the nineteenth century, Britain entered the twentieth century partially disabled in the fight for economic modernisation.

The cultural aversion to business, science and modernity may indeed be a key virus in the much discussed post-Second World War 'British disease' of slow growth and relative economic decline, despite a variety of economic regimes, from the Keynesian welfare state experiment through to the 1980s economic neo-liberalism of Margaret Thatcher. The explanation for Britain's economic problem may not lie in the choice of economic strategy and policy, but in deeper cultural problems at the heart of British society.

A 'cultural explanation' may be all the more in order when foreign experiences are analysed. For example, the United States and Germany are at opposing poles of the Western economic debate. Whereas American economic philosophy tends to emphasise classical capitalist nostrums of minimal government and maximal individualism, the post-war German state sees a positive role for the state in industry, and promotes a framework of dirigism and corporatism. Both are more economically successful than Britain. And both these republics possess a modern democratic political culture where the governing ideology does not resist commercial values. The thorough-going American bourgeois experience (translated to West Germany after the Second World War) was able to develop because, from the American revolution onwards, there was no feudal political template to constrict it. In the United States the people owned the state, or at least they thought they did.

The ideology of ordinariness

The cultural aversion of the British to business, commerce and trade (and its reflection in a bias towards aristocracy and land) has translated itself over time into a more contemporary anti-success and anti-merit ethic. We can see this ethic at work in all walks of life, working equally against apparently pushy professionals, thrusting entrepreneurs or excessively clever politicians, and providing one of the primary reasons for the failure of Britain to establish anything resembling a meritocratic system of values, a society which encourages talent and achievement. Many policy-makers (including modern Conservatives) tend to locate the germs of uncompetitiveness in the realm of high tax rates, union power and sloppy and insensitive management. But these are the symptoms only of the disease of generalised cultural resistance to talent and merit.

The attractions of a culture of anti-meritocracy are obvious: anyone who does well by reason of effort and talent automatically becomes a threat to the esteem of those who do not. The old English class system kept the talented in their place, and in contemporary Britain monarchy can serve the same purpose. After all, a king or a queen does not secure his or her position by open competition, by virtue of work, talent or achievement – indeed, monarchs have historically been associated not only with lack of talent and merit, but also with idleness, stupidity, frivolity and corruption. A major theme of English radicalism and republicanism – from Milton and the supporters of the Commonwealth onwards – has been the projection of monarchs as unworthy recipients of others' toil. Take the republican poet Shelley, who in 1812 could write:

> Whence, think'st thou, kings and parasites arose?
> Whence that unnatural line of drones, who heap
> Toil and unvanquishable penury
> On those who build their palaces, and bring their daily
>   bread?[15]

Republicanism in North America, as it developed in the eighteenth century, drew on the English radical tradition. Hence the historian Gordon Wood can argue that during the 1790s Jeffersonian republicans like Matthew Lyon labelled the Federalist gentry as men brought up in 'idleness, dissipation and extravagance' and Abraham Bishop attacked 'monarchy' for having 'courtiers' and 'sinecures' and men receiving 'princely estates for trifling services'. By comparison, the new republican society being established believed in work. Indeed, Wood argues that 'productive labour now came to be identified with republicanism and idleness with monarchy'.[16]

Perhaps nothing separated early-nineteenth-century Americans more from their British cousins than did their rejection of the idea of a ruling class, and the importance they placed upon labour and everyone's participation in it. In America, wrote Theodore Sedgwick, 'to live without some regular employment or industry is not reputable'.[17] Exactly the opposite view was held in the monarchies of old Europe, particularly by the English aristocracy. For them, leisure and idleness – as long as they were backed up by unearned inherited wealth – were the fountain springs of repute and honour.

This aristocratic disdain for talent, merit and success is still alive and well in contemporary Britain, and is exemplified by Britain's royal family, who, whatever else they are, are certainly not exemplars of an educated elite. Their own personal educational qualifications and achievements are, for a family with so many resources, simply mediocre. Nor do they provide a role model for talent and achievement, or for earned and uninherited business enterprise. They have added little to the world of arts or science. Indeed, a monarch and a 'royal family', virtually by definition, can act as role models only for the lifestyle of inheritance – exactly contrary to the needs of an enterprise or meritocratic society.

If monarchy is not meritorious, then maybe, as some monarchists argue, it is representative of changing social mores: the very randomness of its selection represents 'ordinary' family life, including the 'ordinary' breakdown of the family. Yet even if monarchy is 'ordinary' in this sense (it certainly isn't in the sense of the resources and opportunities it has at its disposal), is it the best mechanism for elevating 'ordinary' values into the symbols of governance? Would not a presidency be filled by just as authentically 'ordinary' a family, elected, nominated or selected at random – a family which would have their term of office limited by law, after which another 'ordinary' family could take over?

As well as this anti-success ethic, Britain's monarchical culture, and what R. H. Tawney described as 'the lingering aroma of the aristocratic legend', is also responsible for the deadly ideology of paternalism which still infuses modern British life.

We can see the paternalist impulse at work in the very governance of Britain, through institutions which themselves took root before the democratic age. We can see it also in the continuing atmosphere of *noblesse oblige* which infuses so much charitable work and even attitudes towards the welfare state. We can see it too in the paternalistic politics of upper-class socialists and high Tory Conservatives who still view the political life of the country as a relationship between rulers and ruled. All that is needed, they would maintain, is to get the relationship right; there is nothing wrong with an 'Upstairs-Downstairs', top-down society that a little bit of 'trust' can't put right.

'Trust' (between lord and serf, king and subject) was the glue which kept feudal society together. Yet stability in modern democratic societies no longer rests upon this paternalist idea – instead, the watchwords are consent and accountability. Even so, the reaction of Buckingham Palace to its slide in public support in 1992 exhibited all the old paternalist reflexes expected from monarchy. The Queen was said to believe that 'the problems confronting the monarchy are symptomatic of a breakdown of the *trust*, once deeply held by the public, in the institutional pillars of the nation'. And a courtier said, 'people continue to claim Britain is riddled with class. It is not. But the cement in our society is *trust*.'[18]

There are costs attached to this stubborn paternalist inheritance, not the least of which is its tendency to make babies of us all. Indeed, republican advocates have often suggested that monarchy induces – or perhaps even represents – childlike sensibilities:

> Since the king was the 'paterfamilias of the nation', to be a subject was to be a kind of child, to be personally subordinated to a paternal dominion. In its starkest theoretical form, therefore, monarchy, as Americans later came to describe it, implied a society of dependent beings, weak and inferior, without autonomy or independence, easily cowed by the pageantry and trappings of a patriarchal king.[19]

Perhaps the centuries of 'paterfamilias' paternalism may help explain why so many Britons dream about the Queen, or Princess Diana, or Prince Charles. There is a primitive, childlike quality in the belief that royals are not really human. This childish sensibility helps explain why sections of British opinion should have been so offended by the action of the Australian Prime Minister, Paul Keating, when, during the 1992 royal visit to Australia, he allowed his arm – very tentatively – to hover around the royal waist as he guided the Queen through the crowds and introduced her to the waiting dignitaries. What was essentially a human gesture, from one human being to another, was seen as defiling the sacred!

Yet the most damaging aspect of paternalism is the toll it has taken on the system of government. Among the Western nations, the British are perhaps the least educated on the merits of separated powers and multiple power centres. For instance, the legacy of paternalism has instilled the idea that there is one 'single authority', one 'official' line that needs to be followed – a 'single' royal family setting standards, a 'single' established Church acting as the 'single conscience of the nation', a 'single' branch of government that needs to be obeyed. The virtue of pluralism – of separate, competing and conflicting power centres – has still not become properly established in the contemporary British mind.

4·The Wrong Constitution

That old rascal Walter Bagehot once asserted that when you put before the mass of mankind the question, 'will you be governed by a King or will you be governed by a constitution?' the enquiry comes out thus – will you be governed by something you understand or will you be governed in a way you do not understand.[1] Apart from the essay in paternalism this reveals, the intriguing point about it is that the truth is exactly the other way round. It is not a constitution (by which Bagehot means a written constitution) that is mysterious, but 'kingship', or monarchy, which – apart from its absolutist variety (which Bagehot was not advocating) – is unknown and unknowable.

Only two states in the world – both of them monarchies – possess an unwritten constitution: the British royal-state and the Kingdom of Saudi Arabia. The problem – for both Brits and Saudis – is that no one, not even the most insistent 'subject', can ever know the basic rules of the game, the rules under which he or she lives (and dies). The enquiring (and uppity) British subject wanting a copy of the country's rules will scour the British Museum or the British Library or the Library of the House of Commons in vain. He or she will be 'politely but firmly' told that no such document exists – and, probably, that this mystery is part of the essence of being 'English'. George Dangerfield, in one of the more vociferous tributes to olde constitutionalism, written as late as the 1930s, has argued that such obscurantism is 'good for you':

> To reform the House of Lords meant to set down in writing a Constitution which for centuries has remained happily unwritten, to conjure a great ghost into the narrow and corruptible flesh of a code [the echo here is of the old hatred for the Napoleonic code] ... Materialised this spectral Constitution would have been a very monster, bearing a horrid mixture of features, from Norman French to early Edwardian ... a monster which existed on the principle that every grievance had a remedy ...[2]

To *know* the constitution is not to *love* it. Indeed, such knowledge might actually corrupt and deprave British subjecthood, and introduce into our happy maypole-dancing island 'horrid' foreign monsters.

How, then, is the wretched persistent subject, assuming he or she is willing to take the risk, to find out about the British constitution, when even prime ministers and lord chancellors and the Queen herself have no such ready knowledge? Indeed, during a 'constitutional crisis' the whole country remains in the dark. And with no constitutional court to help out, everyone is forced to rely upon the so-called 'constitutional experts' who appear on the screens and in the newspapers to 'reveal' to a waiting public some definitive answers.

'I doubt it would be constitutional', 'There is nothing unconstitutional about it', 'Constitutionally speaking there is no problem': such is the public gossip of the learned constitutional sages, who, during periods of uncertainty and crisis, and in the absence of a properly constituted court, tend to form opinion. And unhappily (for such is the constitution of an *ancien régime*) these answers can only be unauthoritative, opinionated, ambiguous and numerous. Lord St John of Fawsley, Conservative Lord Blake and the political scientist Philip Norton all, in their differing ways, make stout-hearted attempts to decipher the undecipherable. Yet none of them – like their immediate predecessors Dicey, Bagehot, Jennings, Mackintosh – can agree; and all we are left with is mystery.

Of course, in the absence of a document, and a court to interpret it, the hard political reality is that the constitution of the royal-state bends to the will and convenience of the existing major players. In any constitutional crisis the Queen herself, the Prime Minister, perhaps a cabinet minister or two, perhaps the Archbishop of Canterbury (and maybe the leader of the Opposition), together with that crucial functionary the political adviser to the monarch, will try to settle the matter. Thus it was without reference to any court or document, or to established rules of governance, that it was decided in 1992, by the Queen after 'consulting' the Prime Minister, that she would pay some taxes – those that she chose to.

The excessive cult of secrecy is another aspect of the 'obscurantist' impulse at the heart of the British royal-state. Britain is certainly ahead of its fellow uncodified monarchy, Saudi Arabia, in providing its subjects with access to government information. Yet it lags behind many others – particularly its Western counterparts. The British Parliament still refuses to pass a Freedom of Information Act, and British scholars still labour under an information system that denies them access to certain public records for thirty years – and even after thirty years, for periods up to 100 years, documents can still remain closed to public inspection by something known as a 'Lord Chancellor's Instrument' often invoked on 'grounds of personal sensitivity'.[3]

Like the unwritten constitution itself, the royal-state's cult of secrecy is derived directly from the monarchical past:

> The main difference between the United Kingdom and other countries, as far as freedom of information or access legislation is concerned, is to be found in the fundamental characteristic of Britain's unwritten constitution ... Add to this the observation from D. C. Rowat's comparative survey of administrative secrecy in developed countries, that 'Governments inherited the principle of administrative secrecy from the period of absolute monarchy in Europe, when the King was in control of all information released about government', and a good foundation is laid for

understanding the present position with regard to open government in the United Kingdom.[4]

'We, the people'?

In Britain 'the people' ... what John Stuart Mill called 'the entire aggregate of the community' – do not own their own government. Instead the state (the royal-state of monarch, Lords and Parliament) owns them.[5] In the constitutional theory of republican America and France, by contrast, 'we, the people' protected by fundamental human rights, created the government, and as part of this act of creation ceded power to it. In this sense, government, no matter how overweening or intrusive, is ultimately 'theirs'. They are freeholders. In the British royal-state, by contrast, the people are tenants, or at best leaseholders with long leases.

This sense of the British people having no real stake in their own country (even in its history) has been a consistent theme of radicals. It was a major preoccupation of the intellectual life of A. J. P. Taylor, whose approach to history, according to the historian Norman Stone, was 'that the rising well-being of the people mattered more than anything else – more than battles, peers, archbishops, Oxford colleges, the Empire', and who also believed that the people were thwarted by a particularly closed establishment, what he called 'The Thing'.[6] This is a view no longer restricted to progressive intellectuals:

> They [the Americans] also know that America is their country. It belongs to them. All their history, their teaching, ideology, literature and laws tell them so. The rules and the laws are made for them ... Britain, we know, doesn't belong to us. We don't know who it does belong to, but it's certainly not the people – that's why our laws treat us as nuisances and America treats its people as citizens; that's why its government is open with its people and ours keeps secrets.[7]

Anthony Sampson echoes this point when he argues that

'the continuous role of the Crown . . . the royal crest in the courts of justice, the crown on the civil servant's briefcase, the royal opening of parliament, the prime minister's weekly visit to the palace' serves as the country's substitute for popular sovereignty, and that 'the American alternative of "we, the people" still seems an ocean away.'[8]

But, if the people do not own the state, who, or what, does? For the answer, we must return to Dicey's formulation of 'the Crown in Parliament' – a form often referred to as 'parliamentary sovereignty'. One of Britain's premier political scientists, W. H. Greenleaf, argues that parliamentary sovereignty 'derives from ancient roots [and] is curiously linked . . . with theories about absolute monarchy and the divine right of kings. Just as the notion of a power which could (in Bodin's well-known phrase) give orders to all and receive none from them shifted from emperor to pope to king, so it could be assumed by an assembly.'[9]

What happened in Britain was that the royal-state, never overthrown in the name of the people (not even during the limited duration of Cromwell's Commonwealth), transformed itself over time from a state based upon the 'divine right of kings' into a modern-looking system in which 'the Crown in Parliament' was sovereign, all the time retaining the legal position of the state (against which subjects have no entrenched rights) as absolute, and absolutist. In Britain, quite literally, the Crown in Parliament owns not only the state but also the people who live in it.

At no time during the centuries of development of British government has there been a compact, a founding document, between rulers and ruled, between the people and the state. The royal-state has never established the entrenched rights which go with the republican notion of citizenship, even though it is these 'inalienable' rights which produce the sense in the individual of possessing a 'stake' in the country, and in the system.

The absence of any stake in the British system reveals itself in a thousand different ways – from the very limited spread of share and land ownership to the peculiarly (and uniquely) British form of 'ownership' known as 'leasehold', whereby people who buy flats in many of Britain's major cities and towns (and who raise mortgages on them) do not, in fact, 'own' these dwellings in the normal sense of ownership: after a specified number of years the 'owner' finds that they revert to a large 'estate', often owned by a titled individual such as the Duke of Westminster, who in February 1993 resigned from the Tory Party over the Leasehold Reform Bill, which made its way through Parliament in 1992–3 and introduced a new term, 'commonhold', which allowed some leaseholders to buy freehold rights.

More generally, this lack of a stake in Britain may help to explain how 'the British disease' of deference and general unassertiveness took hold. Those excluded from the action, treated as extras, are likely to go one of two ways: either into a strident rebellion, or, alternatively, into a quiet, unstressed acquiescence. And while this is not to rule out popular opinion as a determinant of British public policy (popular opinion will work its will in Britain, if not to the extent seen in other contemporary Western polities, then at least to some degree), it must be understood that the key point about popular will is that it is meant to serve a function, play a role, 'take its part' in the political life of the country – but *not* to determine it!

Royal-state constitutional 'theory' – which sees the Crown as the template, existing prior to and separate from the people – certainly sees a role for public opinion, but only in limited terms. For example, one function for the people might be thought to be to *participate*. The constitutional historian S. B. Crimes has argued that 'the basic notions of the duty of the subjects to participate in government . . . were characteristic features of the medieval polity'.[10] Yet in royal-state ideology such participation is only in government, not in the state itself, for the state is eternal and mystical, not conducive to democratic control.

Over the centuries, the royal-state has allowed for ever greater participation by the people in the realm of government. The House of Commons is now elected by universal suffrage, although only every four to five years or so. Yet that key constitutional nostrum has remained: the state *grants* (often gracefully, sometimes gracelessly) the people additional powers, and *concedes* democratic advances, while remaining the fount, not only of honour, but of authority. What is more, Britain's evolutionary development has allowed the people only into the lower (sic) House, not into either of the remaining corners of the constitutional triangle.

This unsavoury (yet subtle) top-down constitutional ideology was deciphered by an American citizen who wrote to the *Spectator* in 1940 to argue that Britain was essentially a paternalist polity rather than a democracy. 'Democracy', he argued, 'must stand on a different basis from something which is grudgingly given by a conciliating upper class to classes which are hard pressing . . . It must be of the people before it can be by it or for it.'[11] Indigenous British dissenters, radical liberals and republicans have also isolated this lack of popular sovereignty as the key inadequacy of Britain's constitution. Even A. V. Dicey was to admit this shortcoming, positing in his arguments in favour of referenda that the time had arrived for 'the formal recognition' of popular sovereignty – 'a principle which, in fact if not in theory, forms part of our constitutional morality'.[12]

In *The Rights of Man*, Tom Paine locked horns on the issue with his great philosophic adversary, the high Tory Whig, Edmund Burke:

> Mr. Burke will not, I presume, deny the position I have already advanced; namely, that governments arise, either out of the people or over the people. The English government is one of those which arose out of a conquest, and not out of society, and, consequently, it arose over the people; and though it has been much modified from the opportunity of circumstances since the time of William the Conqueror, the country has never yet regenerated itself, and is therefore without a constitution.[13]

Whether or not the royal-state was, as Paine suggests, born out of conquest, or alternatively can be viewed as a product of indigenous evolutionary development, the fact remains that it has successfully excluded any idea of popular self-determination.

Apart from the upheaval in the 1640s, none of the climacterics of English and British social and political history has involved an attempt to establish a regime of popular sovereignty — even in name, or symbolically. In 1215 Magna Carta was a charter 'granted' by the king to the nobles, with no idea of the people involved at all. Following the regicide in the seventeenth century, in what was a sharp and real discontinuity in the state, it was Parliament (and then the Lord Protector), not the people, which became the focus of authority. In 1688, following a period of real crisis for the state, Parliament (true to its location within the structures of the royal-estate), rather than ushering in a written constitution based upon the principle of popular sovereignty, instead installed a foreign king. The 1832 Reform Act was 'granted' to the emerging middle classes by the nobility; and in the age of democracy, the restructuring of the House of Lords within the royal-state apparatus in the Parliament Act of 1911 was, after much agitation, still 'granted' by Lords and monarch. Even in the early 1990s, with talk of a republic in the air, so all-embracing is the royal-state that a wholly new system of governance can be envisaged only as part of yet another gracious concession — perhaps by the Queen, as a final act. For citizens to demand it, organise for it, and implement it, still remains positively un-English.

The sad fact is that the phrase 'we, the people' has about as much resonance in contemporary British political culture as 'we, the Lords'. Although the direct political power of aristocracy has declined over the twentieth century, its world, described so superbly by the British historian David Cannadine, in his chronicle of its decline, still lives on, in miniature certainly, but with a considerable pull at the very wealthiest and highest social levels in contemporary society.[14] And although the days when everyone 'loved a lord' may have gone, the old upper-class stereotypes still possess a certain allure — particularly to advertisers and glossy magazines. Indeed, a foreigner reading the British mass print media might be forgiven for believing that the island of Britain was indeed a 'kingdom', inhabited largely by people fawning over lords and ladies. As recently as 1992, one of Britain's more 'progressive' newspaper magazines carried not one but two separate stories about aristocrats, one about the Marquess of Blandford (who had just been released from prison) and the other about David Queensberry, called 'the twelfth Marquess' (the magazine was decidedly more interested in the 'nobility' of the Marquess than his work in ceramics, of which he is a professor).[15] Part of the fascination with nobility in the modern age is no doubt its sheer absurdity. After all, there is something disarmingly bizarre about a system in which it is the automatic right of the new Lord Moynihan, son of a masseuse in the Philippines, to help make the laws which govern a free people just by virtue of being the eldest son of an eldest son of an eldest son.

Nowhere is the reality of R. H. Tawney's 'lingering aroma of the aristocratic legend' more manifest than in the singular fact that on the eve of the twenty-first century there still remains standing nothing less than a fully operative House of Lords – the only 'House of Nobles' left in the few remaining Western countries that are still monarchies. This political representation of heredity is the great umbilical cord linking the old world, based upon political rights of land (passing from father to eldest son), to a 'modern Britain' in which huge tracts of land are still owned by what amounts to a small, caste-like aristocracy. It also reflects the continuing cultural 'authority' possessed by inheritance. In his 1965 Ford Lectures at Oxford, the historian J. H. Plumb argued that in Britain, 'no matter how frequently the constitution may have been reformed, the true anatomy of power, which goes deeper than institutions, remains'; and that this 'true anatomy', the root of the matter, remains to this day 'a political and social authority devolved by inheritance . . . birth still remains a broad highway to power'.[16]

Of course, the political representation of heredity is only one of the problems posed by the House of Lords to a supposedly democratic people. The other is the role in the upper house of the 'lifers', those peers appointed to the rank of Baron for life by Macmillan's Life Peerages Act of 1958. One argument often adduced in favour of these life peers – now, together with their blood-line lordships, comprising almost 1200 law-makers funded by the tax-payer – is that, unlike the whipped Party stalwarts in the Commons, they can bring to law-making a certain independence of spirit. In fact, exactly the opposite is true. The problem is that most of these life peerages are awarded by politicians to those who have spent much of their public life cuddling up to those senior politicians who draw up the lists of preferment. The list of the modern life peers, although containing some men and women of achievement, does not read like a 'Who's Who' of the innovative and daring, but rather is filled with retreads from the green benches in the House of Commons.

Traditionally, it has been the 'buying' of peerages which excited talk of corruption – as when Lloyd George sold seats in the legislature, or, as still happens today, when Party benefactors are rewarded with ermine. Yet the real corruption at the heart of the present upper House system is created not by patronage itself, but by its *prospect*. Rather than introducing into the House of Lords a vein of independence, the existence of a nominated element, particularly if nominated by politicians, helps to enforce the executive's desire to keep the House of Commons pliant and unenquiring.

It is this power of patronage which may hold the key to why the House of Lords still survives. No serious politician ever gives up a lever on power, particularly one which involves some degree of Party loyalty. In this sense, Macmillan's Act, painted at the time as a great step forward, was more a shrewd addition to prime ministerial power. (The politicians in the lower House are also keen not to provide the House of Commons with any competitors; and an elected upper House, by the very fact of its being elected, would do just that.)

The politicians of the lower House (taking their cue from what has now become a settled aspect of public opinion) could simply abolish the hereditary element in the House of Lords, leave the 'lifers' in place, and suffer no loss – either in patronage or by virtue of competition. Yet, intriguingly, they have not. Of course, any attempt simply to remove the hereditary element while keeping the 'lifers' on the constitutional payroll would isolate the monarchy, leaving it standing alone as the one hereditary institution in the country. Such a possibility would have been a primary concern of the Queen during Richard Crossman's attempt to reform the Lords in the 1960s. Indeed, the royal-state survives in part because its various constituent parts (monarchy, hereditary element in the Lords, established Church) all fit together and protect each other. Tampering with one makes the others vulnerable.

The fact is that the aristocracy in Britain serves a highly practical purpose: as a cover for extremes of wealth, in a country where power lies in land and money – not in the American sense of a general public enjoyment of the good material things in life, but rather in the *ancien régime* sense of protecting the inherited wealth of a super-rich caste attempting, successfully so far, to co-exist with one of the poorest populations in the advanced Western world. In royal-state Britain, the super-rich cannot simply be rich; that would leave them too exposed. Instead, they must also be required to legislate. If the super-rich, like the Duke of Westminster, hold an 'official' social and political position (in a peerage), then the most interesting thing about them becomes not what they own, but the fact that they are titled. Similarly, the most fascinating thing about Britain's richest family – the Windsors – was not (until recently) their wealth, but rather their 'royalness'.

The camouflaging of Britain's egregiously rich beneath a patina of political service will, of course, fail as more and more information becomes available about the sheer extent of the wealth of some of the country's families. Thus, popular exposés, such as the *Sunday Times*'s annual '100 Richest People' (a feature of American life for many decades), can only help forward the day when in Britain the super-rich are treated as what they are: the super-rich, without the added nobility!

The thought of the abolition of the House of Lords no longer arouses the primitive emotions of a reactionary class. Lord Rosebery's outburst in 1911, when the Lords was under threat, that the country was facing 'the end of all, the negation of faith, of family, of property' would not, this time, be heard in the land. It might, though, be heard in the inner sanctums of the House of Windsor, for whom it functions as one of the crucial underpinnings of its own legitimacy.

Lords spiritual

Should the House of Lords be abolished it will no longer be able to play host to the Archbishop of Canterbury and those other twenty-five Anglican bishops who sit on its red benches and help determine the laws of the British state. This 'mixing' of Church and state is the stuff of 'establishment', yet the bizarre sight of 'bishops in the legislature' is only one, somewhat lowly aspect of the special relationship between Church and state. Another is the role played by Parliament in approving the rules, doctrine and theology of the Church, and by Downing Street in picking the Archbishop of Canterbury (from a list of two). Yet the 'crowning' relationship is between monarch and Church, Queen and Archbishop. It is as the 'Supreme Governor' of the Church that the Queen appoints the Archbishop of Canterbury; and in a return compliment the Archbishop is the one who 'crowns' and 'anoints' the monarch during the coronation ceremony.

This incestuous relationship between spiritual and temporal (which also extends in Scotland to the Church of Scotland) not only violates the crucial Western liberal democratic principle that Church and state should be separated, but represents, in theory at least, a fusion not seen outside some of the most theocratic Islamic states. Mature democracies take great care to draw the line between Church and state, certainly at the constitutional level. The Americans (in the First Amendment to the Constitution) state that 'Congress shall make no law respecting an establishment of religion'; the French (from 1905, and again in the constitution of the Fifth Republic) proclaim their republic to be 'secular'; and the Germans (in their Basic Law) shun the notion of a state religion or church. Even in Catholic Concordat countries, such as Ireland, Spain and Italy (where there is now no question of the Pope anointing the head of state!), there is formally at least a looser relationship between the Church and state than exists in secular, Protestant Britain.

This special role of the Church of England in the higher reaches of the constitution is not only an affront to the 'separation' principle, it also represents that strain of English paternalism in which a single 'official' authority, or 'official' family, or 'official' Church, sets norms and demands respect. It amounts to an unspoken assumption that there exists a single community needing established spiritual guidance – enthroning the Church of England as the 'official', self-proclaimed 'conscience of the nation'.

Mark Santer, Bishop of Birmingham and one of the prelates who has already expressed himself publicly in favour of disestablishment, has suggested that:

> The worst thing about the special status of the Church is the corruption of spirit it encourages. We collude implicitly with the notion that 'Anglican' equals 'really English', thereby reducing our fellow Christians to the status of inferior citizens.[17]

Quite so. But the argument goes beyond Christians: it is not only Baptists or Methodists or Congregationalists or Free Presbyterians who think of themselves as citizens, as nationals, as 'English', but also Jews, atheists, Muslims, Hindus, Buddhists, and all those who have no particular commitment to any one faith.

In trying to explain how the royal-state could get itself into this imbroglio, apologists look to Britain's inheritance. The British, like everyone else, are lumbered with historical baggage. The 'special arrangement' that started with the political event of Henry's Reformation and solidified over the centuries as the 'established Church' became a symbol of the country's Protestantism, and a defining distinction between the British state and Roman Catholic Europe, is simply a fact of life – or is it? For surely there have been many opportunities to 'disestablish' the Church. Welsh disestablishment was one of them; any of the twentieth-century coronations were others. And the arguments have been well rehearsed, as there has always – in the twentieth century – been a body of opinion in the Church itself and in Parliament which has favoured breaking the link and setting both state and Church free.

The reason the leadership of the Church, certainly unhappy with having their affairs controlled by Parliament and their Archbishop selected by Downing Street, baulks at the final hurdle is their belief that the Christian position in the country would suffer as a result. Disestablishment, for all its stirrings of radical memory, is not a hot subject outside the Synod. Just as Britain's trade union leaders have still not recovered from being dismissed from their role in the state – from Downing Street's 'tea and sandwiches' – so there is no reason why prelates should not feel the same way.

Disestablishment of the Church would not only abolish one of the most cherished of Elizabeth Windsor's roles (as 'Supreme Governor'), but would also remove the crucial 'anointing' of a new sovereign, one of the royal rituals taken most seriously by the Queen. Defending the royal-state is like an elaborate war-game, but one in which defeat on any one front (the union between England and Scotland, the House of Lords, the established Church, the unwritten constitution) leads straight to the capital (the monarchy itself) and the undermining of the whole edifice.

Orders of Ruritania

Of course, while the exact relationship between the British state and the 'Lords Spiritual and Temporal' is of little interest to the average punter, one area where Britain's constitution does touch the lives and aspirations of considerable numbers of Britons is the honours system. It is the point of contact between the royal-state and the people, and its *modus operandi* is highly sensitive.

In 1992 John Major, surprised to discover that honours were still awarded according to social 'rank', attempted to focus debate upon 'who gets what' in the honours game. As part of the drive towards a 'classless society' Major established a governing principle: that merit (or bravery) should become the sole criterion for awards, and that no particular category of honour would be reserved for particular social classes. Thus, in the rather tame reform of honours announced in March 1993, Major abolished the distinction between the British Empire Medal (for working-class, blue-collar people) and the Member of the British Empire (MBE) medal for more socially elevated persons.

Major's determination to pursue such a seemingly small point dealt something of a body blow to one of the central postulates of the royal-state: the recognition, indeed the assertion, of social hierarchies and 'ranks'. Yet Major's putative reform still left intact the *character* of the honours bestowed by the royal-state on its subjects. It was the redolent and pugnacious antiquity of these honours that enhanced Britain's 'painted folklore', its 'glamour of backwardness', and thus reinforced its deadly class system.

The very vocabulary of available titles speaks volumes about the country's attachment to the past. There is the Order of the Garter, the Order of the Thistle, the Order of the Bath, the Order of St Michael and St George, and, leaving Ruritania and coming right up to date, the imperial titles of the Royal Victorian Order and the Order of the British Empire. These awards produce 'Knights', 'Dames', 'Companions' and, for good measure, real-life 'Commanders'.

In a sense it is a great tribute to the British appreciation of magic that 'ordinary people' – like Whitehall under-secretaries – can suddenly and mystically become transformed into 'Commanders of the British Empire', when what exactly they command remains a mystery and what empire they run is unstated. In the case of the peerage, this transformation becomes, literally, an 'elevation'. (To what remains unclear, though the suggestion is that a higher plane of existence comes with closer proximity to the royal family.) This elevation is made real by a mid-life (or late-life) name change. Britain is the only country in the world in which people change their names – from ordinary ones such as George Thomas into extraordinary ones like 'Lord Tonypandy' – in order to sit in the legislature.

Are all these garbs and garters and titles truly 'harmless fun'? Simply a dash of colour and pageant in an otherwise drab world? The kind of exhibitionism which does no harm, and offends only the 'dour republican'? Well, yes; but also, no. For the sad fact is that for many Britons the honours system is no fun at all, but a matter to be taken seriously, with the exact position in the final honours pecking-order often the subject of lifetime anxiety and neurosis, the weight of acquired grandiosity requiring an added crutch to bear it, rather than conferring any genuine dignity or nobility. David Carlton sees these honours making sense only, 'if at all, when we really were seen as Lords of Humankind. Now that we have become one of the poorest, and arguably the most brutish, of countries in the advanced world we court only ridicule by retaining such titles on any official basis.'[18]

The honours game of the royal-state is more than a simple public recognition awards system. Rather, as well as reinforcing the country's peculiar sense of importance, it legitimises ancient class sensibilities – and in the process sanctifies the idea that achievement is not enough, that even in the twentieth century achievement cannot speak for itself. While captains of industry fall over themselves to be called 'sir', and trade unionists and academics manoeuvre for peerages, the money made, the business created, the invention produced or the book written assumes little value in itself. The ultimate prize is something much more precious: the medieval title, a position in an eternal social hierarchy, the opportunity to parade a kind of social apartness based upon an illusion of nobility, or at least gentrification.

Why is it that American, German or French business leaders don't seem, as so many of their British counterparts do, to need these cute titles in front of their names? Why do American, German and French politicians not feel the need to spend their sunset years being called 'Lord this or that' and sit unelected in an upper House? Why do American, German or French artists, actors and literary figures seem to possess no desire to end their days bathing in the glow of some state-invested title? Perhaps it all comes down to a widespread social insecurity on the part of Britain's business and professional elite, a need to be accepted in a culture in which achievement is still not valued, to find a resting-place in an officially sanctioned social niche deriving from pre-commercial times – knowing who is above and below you, and caring about it.

Whether we British will ever rid ourselves of our love affair with 'gongs' and titles is a question that can only be answered by the Party leaders and whips – those who manipulate the system, and derive power from it. It may be asking too much for them to give away the patronage that the honours system bestows on them. It may also be asking too much for them to stand up to our title-loving monarch and remove the royal right to hand out titled largesse. Although only a few of the honours bestowed are nowadays in the personal gift of the Queen, the culture of blatant patronage, with all its decadent and degenerative side-effects, is a direct product of the royal-state. And, conversely, the bestowing of these gifts, whatever the source of recommendation which produced them, redounds directly to the benefit of the monarch. The host of political hacks, military officers, tame academics, Whitehall mandarins and Conservative Party fund-raisers who mill around with their families in the forecourt of Buckingham Palace, parading their new baubles before the cameras, have through these investiture ceremonies been given the opportunity to affirm their loyalty – or, more appropriately, their fealty – to the royal system.

Thus, in another of these symbiotic relationships so crucial to the survival of the British monarchy, an honours system theoretically intended to reward achievement has in practice ended up as yet another strut propping up the royal edifice.

A right royal constitution

Britain's ancient royal-state (with its weak lower House, its monarchy, Lords, established Church and feudal titles) is not inadequate simply because it is old-fashioned, allowing the country only to *adapt* to the modern democratic age, not to be *determined* by it. The real problem is the commitment to antiquity – the belief that all virtue lies in a traditional, evolutionary system – which in modern Britain serves somehow to obviate the need to think about ideas and principles, let alone

74

incorporate them into the rules. Yet ideas have consequences: they have informed and infused not only the constitutions but the political life of most of the West's great democracies.

Take, for instance, the idea of 'rights'. Rights are the very bedrock of modern democracy. They establish the individual as supreme over the state, they protect minorities, and they serve to limit the intrusiveness and arbitrariness of government. Ever since Tom Paine raised the standard with his *Rights of Man*, most modern democracies have incorporated this powerful liberal idea into the very fabric of their constitutional arrangements. Most, but not all, since Paine's own homeland remains an exception. Of course, the modern British are certainly a free people in any realistic sense of the term. Yet the fact remains that their rights are not *entrenched*. They possess no constitutional safeguards for their liberties, and consequently their rights remain at the disposal of the authorities, the transient interest of the media and the whims of public opinion. What is given can be taken away.

Of course, on the issue of entrenching a Bill of Rights, the royal-state is incapacitated. It is not that its apparatus is against the idea. After all, 'Her Majesty's Government' signed both the United Nations Convention on Human Rights and the European Convention on Human Rights, and it has even agreed to an enforceable Bill of Rights for Hong Kong. The problem is that to introduce such a Bill for Britain would involve a new written constitution. As Lord Hailsham has argued:

> Surely if it is to be worth the paper it is written on, a Bill of Rights must be part of a written constitution in which the powers of the legislature are limited and subject to review by the courts. Otherwise it will prove to be a pure exercise in public relations.[19]

A new constitution would involve nothing less than discarding the old, unwritten, royal-state constitution. Thus a huge irony emerges, in which the country which pioneered the liberal conception of politics cannot implement it, and the nation which has on its books Magna Carta and the 1689 Bill of Rights is disabled from entrenching a modern version.

In the summer of 1991 John Patten, as Home Office Minister, made an official foray in the constitutional reform debate:

> It is far better that rights are determined and protected through elected representatives, sensitive to the rights of the individual and to the community as a whole, than by necessarily and properly isolated judges. To transfer such power to judges is to transform power to too few ... [Parliament] unlike the courts is a deliberative body, able to discuss and resolve tensions between the needs of the individual and the community as a whole ... This is the best mechanism for maintaining the balance that is essential to the health of our community; and it has contributed to the success of what is an extraordinarily liberal and tolerant country.[20]

The problem with Patten's analysis is that he is conjuring up a Parliament that no longer exists, even though it may have in the seventeenth century, and possibly even in the nineteenth. Today, the House of Commons bends and trembles before an over-mighty executive, has few rights of inquiry and investigation, and is anyway essentially a ratifying body whose *raison d'être* is both to create (out of its majority) and to support Her Majesty's government. Patten was on stronger ground when in another section of the same lecture he argued that a regime of rights was best protected by a sympathetic political culture, arguing that 'we need to consider our political culture first – it underpins everything constitutional – before looking at the various proposals for change'.[21] However, modern British Conservatives themselves – from Thatcher to Major – are often in the forefront of the argument that Britain's political culture is extraordinarily backward: resistant to enterprise and competition, as well as far too deferential and unassertive. The Tory MP George Walden has suggested that the concept of citizenship is 'far too weakly developed' in Britain, in part because of this deferential culture.[22] Perhaps modern Conservatives need to reflect upon the possibility that cultural change may be induced not just by an enterprise revolution, but also by a rights revolution.

Labour and the Liberal Democrats too have shifted, recognising that real radical politics no longer amounts to steering their supporters towards nationalisation and public ownership, but rather entails a programme for opening up and democratising Britain's pre-modern institutions and society. Increasingly, both Opposition parties are placing the need for a Bill of Rights at the very centre of this process.

The other great organising principle of Western liberal democracy – the separation of powers – is also impossible to attain while Britain continues with its unwritten royal-state constitution.

Throughout most of the Western world it is now axiomatic that freedoms are protected, not just by formal rights, but also by the crucial underpinning of a plurality of power centres. By competing with each other these institutions set up a system of checks and balances which prevents any one of them from becoming so powerful that it threatens the rights of the individual. Such a separation is at the heart of the most recent federal constitution, the German Basic Law, where, for instance, federal and state (*Länder*) authorities are balanced off against each other. In the United States' constitution the separations are so clearly defined that the President, Congress and the Supreme Court are virtually invited to engage in conflict. Conversely, it is the mark of a totalitarian system that only one power centre exists – in the case of the communists, the single authority of 'the Party', which pervaded and invaded the lives of its citizens.

'All would be lost,' wrote Montesquieu, the great modern proselytiser of the idea of the separation of powers, 'if the same man or the same ruling body, whether of nobles or of the people, were to exercise these three powers, that of law-making, that of executing the public resolutions, and that of judging crimes and civil causes.'[23] The problem for the British is that, as with the question of a Bill of Rights, the old royal-state constitution simply cannot deliver a system of separated power. Thus, although Montesquieu's great theory of separated powers has had a lasting influence upon Western governance, it didn't take hold in Britain, where 'this theory was opposed in the eighteenth century by the doctrine of the mixed or balanced constitution, in which monarchical, aristocratic and democratic elements were joined and held in equilibrium'.[24]

In the nineteenth century Britain's royal-state marginalised even further the idea of separated powers by coming up with the doctrine -- drawn from the absolutist, centralising and unifying impulses of the idea of Crown and monarchy – of a 'sovereign Parliament'. This theory of 'parliamentary sovereignty' was, of course, propounded by A. V. Dicey in his influential late-nineteenth-century work *Law and Constitution* (where he argued that it was 'the very keystone of the law of the constitution'.[25]) As the nineteenth gave way to the twentieth century, however, 'parliamentary sovereignty' became a sham. On one level, it was theoretically valid. Parliament (by which commentators increasingly meant the House of Commons) was indeed the only institution which could initiate and (with royal approval) pass laws. It was also, without doubt, the creator of an executive (brought into being by a parliamentary majority), and was able to dismiss the executive (by a vote of no confidence). Yet the growth of disciplined and highly organised political parties in the twentieth century meant that the House of Commons simply became a mechanism for supporting the majority Party's executive.

In fact, as the twentieth century progressed, the 'sovereignty of Parliament' (and the pumped-up ceremonial of the House of Commons) was used as a cover for the mammoth growth in the executive power of the British royal-state. As long as the fiction (that the executive was responsible to Parliament) remained intact, then what was fast becoming a highly centralised, executive-dominated state became both tolerable and sellable. Far from separated powers, there was to be no competition between the executive branch and the legislative branch, no competition between the two Houses, no competition between the courts and the other branches. Indeed, power became so centralised and concentrated in the executive (or, for the squeamish, in 'parliamentary sovereignty') that in Britain's polity there are now no *branches* of government at all! Outside the London-based executive (that is, 'the Crown' – the monarch, the Cabinet and government and the civil service), there are no independent entrenched power centres left standing: not in the counties, not in the regions, not in the nations, not in the Commons. The victory of the executive has been complete.

It is no doubt rather apt that, as it comes under increasing pressure to reform itself or clear the decks for the establishment of a republic, the royal-state reverts to an institutional framework so redolent of its absolutist monarchical past. Instead of fostering competition, the twentieth-century British political class has been unable to understand it; instead of encouraging pluralism, they have fallen back upon their long-time love, and vice — the pull of 'sovereignty'.

The idea of pluralism remains a tender plant at the very best of times. In modern society both the pace of technological change and the managerial corporate culture tend to conspire against the absolute imperative of a devolution and diffusion of power. In the political realm the principle and practice of the separation of powers is a well-established mechanism for ensuring basic liberties. Although at present it has no real home in the rules of the royal-state, the increasing assertiveness of a more politically conscious and less reverential society is raising levels of awareness on the issue which cannot bode well for the royal status quo.

5·The Wrong Society

There is something wilfully remote about the Windsors. Elizabeth, shielded from the realities of everyday life in Britain, remains inaccessible to 'her' people. Unlike her North European counterparts she does not mingle with the population or give interviews. Martin Jacques has pointed out that, 'unlike Queen Margrethe of Denmark, you will never bump into her in the local supermarket'.[1] Her children have been sheltered, and their social circle is confined to the gentry or the real and aspiring aristocracy.

In the nineteenth century the royal court played a dual role – as both a crucial part of the state machinery, and the head of what the Victorians called 'society'.[2] Now, at the end of the twentieth century, Britain remains in the same peculiar position, possessing a monarchy which is both part of the state machinery and, arguably because of this fact, immensely important socially.

Of course, the royal family can hardly stand accused of setting the tone for modern personal morality. More likely they follow it. However, on a deeper level the institution of monarchy can only serve to reinforce (and give sanction to) the idea of a hierarchical, ordered and paternalistic society – and is indeed the very hallmark of Britain's persistent and troubling class system.

Britain's insistent sense of class was a constant theme of left-of-centre academics, politicians and writers during the post-Second World War decades. (George Orwell spoke for a generation of these social critics when he asserted that Britain was 'the most class-ridden society under the sun'.) As working-class or lower-middle-class Conservatives like Norman Tebbit and John Major increasingly assumed positions of power, this refrain was also heard from within the Tory establishment, from where criticisms of the monarchy were also increasingly aired. Indeed, John Major made the creation of a 'classless society' his campaign theme during the contest for the Tory leadership in 1990, and subsequently restated it as a goal for his government – even though in so doing he was, perhaps unwittingly, prodding at the Achilles heel of many a traditionalist Tory, whose *raison d'être*, though often unstated, was to perpetuate Britain's class-based society. Moreover, it was somewhat awkward, to say the least, for the leader of the traditional Party of Crown and court to proselytise about social equality in a manner which could obviously open up to debate the whole erstwhile hidden question of monarchy.

There followed much Tory back-tracking. The word went out that the new boy in Downing Street didn't mean to talk about class at all, and certainly didn't want to create a bland and egalitarian society. What Britain needed was something far less terrifying – an 'opportunity society', an 'open society', one 'without barriers'.

This redefinition prompted what amounted to a national debate. By the early 1990s even mainstream Conservatives were beginning to ask what it was that made Britain's class system different. After all, other countries possessed 'north–south' divides, gaps between rich and poor, white-collar and blue-collar workers, disparities between inner city and suburb, and the growth of an 'underclass'. What made the British class system unique?

The answer to this question lies in the sheer antiquity of Britain's class system. Like other advanced nations, the British possess a social structure derived from the history of the industrial revolution (with its often sharp distinctions between capitalists, managers and workers). But what sets Britain apart is not only the persistence into a more 'mature bourgeois' age of these older industrial stereotypes, but also the deadly nostalgia for an ancient culture of 'ranks and orders' drawn from the social hierarchy of the dim and distant medieval past.

This culture retains its life within modern Britain by its presence within national and governmental symbolisms. The legislature, as we have seen, is divided into 'ranks' drawn straight out of the Middle Ages, while the whole socio-political scene is studded with the sharp images of feudalism. This love of an older social order surfaces in a thousand small ways. One such is the continuing literary fascination with the idea of the 'gentleman': 'The Gentleman in Trollope' was the subject of a learned work as late as the early 1980s.[3]) Another is the astoundingly old-fashioned culture of the British military, where even today a frozen, closed world of 'officers' and 'other ranks' pertains. Even British accents and speech patterns still denote 'rank'. We possess the strange conception of an 'official accent' – received pronunciation – in which the cultivated Englishman is actually defined (he's the one who moves his jaws while not swallowing his words whole). Regional accents – Brummie, Scouse, Geordie – are decidedly 'lower drawer'. And 'squire' and 'guv'nor' are still greetings heard on the streets of London. But not only are the British still 'branded on the tongue'; they are also deciphered according to the way they eat and dress. Even that most culturally levelling of activities, sport, has class connotations. Cricket and Rugby Union are for the 'toffs', soccer and Rugby League for the 'proles'.

Not surprisingly, therefore, the British are still a nation of classes cut off from one another both physically and culturally. Although, strangely, we pride ourselves on a single national identity (which is now allegedly under threat from the European union), our classes rarely mix; and most depressing of all, we still cannot talk to one another. Social apartheid still reigns.

Perhaps the most deadly aspect of the nostalgia for an older class sensibility is the toll it takes upon the self-confidence of the peoples of Britain. The sad fact is that British culture actively discourages its people from attaining a high self-image. The standard class explanation has it that in Britain's highly stratified society (where class distinctions are reinforced by official symbolism), the injuries and resentments of those whose class background – based upon economic status, schooling, dress, manners and suchlike – excludes them from Britain's elite power positions are bound to create a generalised low self-esteem. But while there can be little doubt that in Britain self-confidence is indeed associated as much with social characteristics as with personality traits, this low self-regard cannot be explained by class analysis alone, for in Britain the problem of social insecurity is *general*, affecting people in all groups at every level of society.

British political culture actively discourages its people from attaining a high self-image and the self-confidence which flows from it. This contrasts extremely unfavourably with the American social environment, in which individualism, assertiveness and 'aggressiveness' (a term of approbation in the United States) are actively encouraged. The writer and journalist Robert Chesshyre, who has divided much of his time between Britain and North America, observed that American children were different from British in that so many of them were 'launched into life with enormously positive [personal] impulses'.[4]

It may be that the failure of the British to develop similar feelings of self-confidence is a product of the hopelessness (for most of them) of the general economic climate in which, during the twentieth century, they have found themselves. The ability to 'advance oneself in life' through social or geographic mobility, or access to education, has always been difficult and limited, and the British have no 'frontier', or 'west', which could allow even an *imagination* of opportunity. All this was compounded by the loss of Empire, the one thing which the excluded 'working-class' British believed made them exceptional and in which they could take a collective pride. Yet ultimately it is Britain's top-down monarchical and paternalist political culture that must be identified as the culprit. How is it possible to induce self-confidence in a population of 'subjects' devoid of the formal rights of citizenship? As those who in the 1980s sought to create an enterprise culture in Britain might ask: how can a climate of self-confidence and self-esteem be engendered in a country whose official ideology (enshrined in its constitution) derives from the feudal social divisions of king, lord and serf and whose national symbols derive from the inescapable birthright of heredity?

More insidious than the royal-state's role in fostering a lack of social confidence among the British is its base exploitation of this weakness. The British form of corruption does not involve money; rather, it amounts to the manipulation by the royal-state of the widespread need for social acceptance and recognition. If American evangelists 'prey upon the weak', then our honours system exploits the same human frailty in the secular English. It is as if the applicant is told, 'You don't have to pay, but if you obey me, then although you may not get into heaven, you will certainly get into the club.'

The lack of social confidence induced in its subjects by the culture of the royal-state goes deep and wide. Hardly any British soul is unaffected. It even afflicts many of Britain's 'Brightest and Best' – the wealth-creators and the meritocrats. Richard Cobden's great quote that 'manufacturers and merchants seem only to desire riches that they may be enabled to prostrate themselves at the feet of feudalism' still – even now – rings true.

The royal-state's political class is particularly open to the need for social acceptance. Take, for instance, a former Prime Minister, Margaret Thatcher, and a former Foreign Secretary and Party leader, David Owen, both of whom in their political careers represented meritocratic values. Neither of these successful ex-politicians needed to accept a peerage for financial reasons; nor do they need to be a member of the upper House in order to secure a platform. Tom Paine's injunction to his fellow subjects to 'walk by the light of their own eyes' may need one more generation in order to be heeded.

This need to be, in some indefinable way, 'acceptable' (at court), is no harmless British – or English – eccentricity. Its consequences have been deadly. Like the archetypal 'self-loathing Jew' who adopts the attitudes and mannerisms of host communities, we can properly detect a 'self-loathing Brit'. How else to explain why so many of the modern British feel that their backgrounds are inadequate (particularly in relation to the 'upper class' and 'royalty')? How else to explain why prime ministers like Margaret Thatcher and other political leaders from ordinary backgrounds, like Roy Jenkins, Cecil Parkinson and Michael Howard, feel so ashamed of their childhood accents that they try to obliterate them? How else to explain the continuing allure of strange historic class eccentricities like Oxbridge high table and judicial wigs among otherwise modern meritocrats? And how else to explain the tendency of the British, no matter how ostensibly radical, to succumb in the end to the joys of class and royalty? Andrew Duncan, a royalist, recounts the story of the greatest of post-war meritocrats, Richard Crossman, who led the failed charge against the House of Lords in the mid-1960s, and whose anti-monarchical sentiments were well honed (he found the Queen 'frightfully horsey'). Evidently Crossman's radical impulses wilted after dinner with the Queen. 'Strange,' remarks Duncan cutely, 'how everyone succumbed in the end' – as though it were inevitable.[5]

Perhaps the best example of British self-loathing is to be found in the constitutional debate about royalty. Monarchists believe that one of their most potent arguments against a republic is the view that no one – but no one – other than the designated hereditary figure would be a satisfactory head of state. Michael Shea, a royal servant, has outlined what he argues is a 'nightmare scenario of a President Thatcher or President Kinnock or Hattersley or Howe or President Kaufman. Let us leave that prospect to the tiny fringe, those latter-day Willie Hamiltons.'[6] What this argument amounts to is the view that a nation of 55 million is unable to come up with anyone who is more appropriate as head of state than someone who is the result of hereditary pot-luck.

The created mentality of low self-esteem has also helped to foster what almost amounts to a national culture of pessimism. It could be glimpsed in the wary cynicism of the 1950s Northern comedian, Al Reid, and in the hopeless braggadocio of East Cheam's Tony Hancock. Of course, self-loathers never win: the world is against them; obstacles are too great; the glass is always half empty (when, in truth, it is half full).

This general attitude of hopelessness plays itself back into the contemporary debate about monarchy, and is reflected in the view that it is hopeless to believe that, as far as the basic structures of the British state are concerned, any change is possible. Thus low self-esteem is accompanied, inevitably, by low aspirations. Britain's inter-war trade-union leader, Ernest Bevin, once lamented the condition of the people 'from whence he came', claiming that the 'working class has been crucified on the poverty of its own desires'. He was referring to the complex of unassertive and unambitious personal attitudes which he saw displayed by the working people of his time, but the point could still be taken at the end of the century, some fifty years after his death.

No matter the prosperity or status into which the modern British are born – they are all still, essentially, allotted an assigned 'place' for life, with only exceptional people being able to break through the social barriers that constantly present themselves. It is this sense of social constrictedness that has encouraged all that is stagnant in British society.

An exclusive society

Perhaps the most damaging of all the social effects of class distinction is a seemingly endemic upper-class English attachment to exclusiveness. On one level this is exhibited in the harmless fetish for clubs – from the grand clubs of Pall Mall to the incestuous dining clubs of young aspirants at university. On another level, and somewhat more insidiously, it has revealed itself in such self-consciously intellectual inter-war networks or coteries as the 'Bloomsbury Nine' and the Cambridge 'Apostles'. The *Times Higher Educational Supplement* commented on the damage wrought to British cultural and intellectual life by this exclusiveness in 1988:

The delight in excluding rather than including which is so characteristic of Britain's national culture has also deeply influenced the patterns of our intellectual life. In some instances this is blighted by an absurd kind of aristocratic privacy. Too many disciplines have clubbable standards which far exceed the standards of discrimination that can be justified by scientific or scholarly criteria. These powerful exclusionary instincts have to be modified if higher education is to reach out into our democracy to touch the whole people.[7]

The 'exclusionary' impulse is primarily the product of a mental and social sensibility (developed mainly in Britain's upper-class males during the period of Empire) which has shunned directness, commitment and engagement. In the process, the upper-class twentieth-century Englishman has developed what appears to be an authoritative manner, which appears, to his compatriots and to foreigners alike, as stand-offish, overly self-contained, indeed almost 'withdrawn' from the world. This type of personality is often exhorted as a virtue, as an aspect of reticence, shyness and a sense of privacy. It has also been lauded as a social necessity – indeed, a 'social good' – in a small and crowded island. Yet it was in the cult of 'rulership' that Britain's upper classes were tutored in repressing their emotions, distance and the withdrawn personality helping to separate (consciously or subconsciously) rulers from ruled. In the end, of course, this rigidity of paternalist manners was self-defeating, creating a rigid disposition among British 'rulers' which was resistant to change, to new ideas, indeed to adaptation itself.

Such a conscious education in separateness was, of course, the lot not only of the generality of public schoolboys, but also of Britain's royal children. Malcolm Muggeridge, who attended Selwyn College, Cambridge, after Selhurst Grammar School, is reported as viewing his fellow students of this era with something approaching contempt – not because they had affairs with one another, but because of their separateness of being:

Public schoolboys, whatever their particular school – from the most famous like Eton, to the most obscure – have a language of their own which I scarcely understood . . . The university, when I was there, was very much a projection of public school life and mores, and a similar atmosphere of homosexuality tended to prevail . . . I emerged unscathed.[8]

George Orwell also wrote eloquently on the subject, in perhaps the most pointed essay ever written from the inside on the terrors and emotional constrictedness of public-school life, 'Such, Such were the Joys'.[9]

The seemingly crimped emotional life of many from this exclusive background also, according to Matthew Parris writing in *The Times*, afflicts 'the Average Briton'. As he puts it: 'The Average Briton is not without intelligence, without a heart or without a soul. It is his unused intelligence, his undeveloped heart and his unacknowledged soul which are the causes of his misery.' He further asks: 'Could there be a couple, could there be a human story, better suited to preside over us as royal ciphers for what we are than the Prince and Princess of Wales?'[10]

Of course, Britain's constitutional system – developed and adapted in the image of this peculiarly separated upper-caste culture – sets the tone in exclusivity, starting at the top with the strange ritual of 'anointing' a new monarch. This is the most sacred and mysterious part of the whole coronation ceremony. And, intriguingly (and appropriately), it takes place in *secret*, with the 'sovereign' shielded from public gaze (including that of the television cameras) by a canopy held aloft by four Knights of the Garter. The Archbishop of Canterbury anoints the new monarch on the hands, the breast and the crown of the head while the choir sings the anthem 'Zadok the Priest'. Then the Archbishop, in a quite extraordinary piece of mumbo-jumbo, declares: 'And as Solomon was anointed King by Zadok the Priest and Nathan the prophet, so be you anointed, blessed and consecrated Queen over the Peoples, whom the Lord your God hath given you to rule and govern . . .'

At the time of her own coronation, Elizabeth II saw fit to accept in its entirety this peculiarly undemocratic and somewhat occultish ceremony – with its echoes of the culture of the 'divine right of kings'. Yet the most interesting aspect of the whole rigamarole is its secrecy, the fact that a head of state

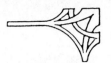

THE
UNWITTING
CATALYST

The ever-dutiful princess, Diana played the game of innocence and became a power in her own right. Her marital fortunes proved to be the catalyst which threatened to unravel the royal-state.

MAKERS
(AND MYTH-MAKERS)
OF THE
MODERN MONARCHY

Above. Prince Albert, the watchful and conscientious husband of the young Queen Victoria, believed that the survival of the monarchy depended on its neutral role, above the political fray. He helped to convert the monarchy from a political into a cultural and social institution. *Facing page, above left.* Walter Bagehot has emerged as the ideologue of the modern monarchy, advocating that distance was power and that no light should be let in on the magic of monarchy. *Above right.* Benjamin Disraeli, flattered his way into Queen Victoria's affections, playing on her ego and imperial sensibilities. Coaxing her back into public life following her husband's death, he helped to forestall a growing unease about the monarchy. *Below.* As ringmaster of the Victorian age, William Gladstone secured the continuing tenure of the monarchy despite being disliked and feared by the bereaved and grieving Queen.

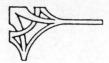

FOUNDER OF THE MODERN MONARCHY

Above. The Great White Queen: Victoria created the symbiotic link between Empire and monarchy. The carefully fostered image of imperial firmness, fairness and enlightenment aided Britain's commercial and economic expansion, so vital to the social and political stability and prosperity of the country up to the 1920s.

Right. The longevity of Victoria, *Regina et Imperatrix*, allowed her politicians to steer the country through the major economic and social changes brought about by the industrial revolution without undue stress on the country's political system.

TRANSITION TO
A KIND OF
MODERNITY

The accession of the former Elizabeth Bowes-Lyon as Queen Consort in 1936 edged the Windsors towards the modern age – less grand than Queen Victoria's, less profligate than Edward VII's and more accessible than George V's.

Above. George VI's stammer and shy disposition encouraged the idea that, although special, royalty was also human.

Right. 'Looking the East End in the eye': George VI and his family enhanced the royal image by remaining in London during the blitz.

Mucking in. The young Princess Elizabeth was presented as a serving ATS during the Second World War. By now fully conscious of the value of public relations, the House of Windsor and its advisors ensured the wide circulation of photographs like this to reinforce the bond between monarchy and people.

The Second World War created a new kind of affection and loyalty towards the British monarchy which, among today's older generation, has survived into the 1990s.

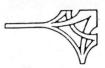

THE NEW
ELIZABETHAN
AGE

The idea of the frail young Elizabeth, propelled unexpectedly on to the throne in 1952, served to release a wave of emotion in favour of the monarchy.

Above. An opportunity to modernise the monarchy, and by extension the climate of British society, was missed in 1953 when the pomp and circumstance of the coronation of Elizabeth II revived nostalgia for an imperial age. In reality, Britain continued its relentless economic and political decline. *Facing page.* The 'family monarchy' was invented under George VI to counteract the effects of the Abdication and to make the concept of royalty more relevant in a democracy.

HAPPY
FAMILIES

Above. The happy family became a fundamental element of the Windsor image. It was an image so assiduously cultivated through photo sessions like this that when reality revealed a different picture, public expectations were disappointed and future constitutional difficulties threatened.

Facing page. The studied casualness of Charles and Diana belied a nuclear family about to explode.

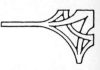

THE
RURITANIAN
CARD

Above. Britain as an historical theme park. The Queen has a good intuitive understanding of pageantry as an important element in the success of the monarchy in Britain. Trooping the Colour offers one of the annual opportunities for the royal-state to renew itself.

Opposite page. In the coronation ceremony the Archbishop of Canterbury intones: 'And as Solomon was anointed king by Zadok the Priest and Nathan the Prophet, so be you anointed, blessed and consecrated King/Queen over the peoples whom the Lord God hath given you to rule over.' Legitimacy is created through mystical rituals which serve to glorify what is merely a constitutional office of state.

The unabashed theatricality of the Ruritanian pageant encompasses even the bit players whose role is all-important in sustaining the fantasies spun by the royal-state.

THE
FEUDAL
HERITAGE

Land ownership is still a basis of power and status in modern Britain. The royal family with its vast estates throughout the kingdom sits at the pinnacle of this system.

Above. In the royal-state the British armed forces take an oath of loyalty to the Queen personally, not to an elected leader, a constitution, Parliament or even the country. Given the absence of a written constitution or any other instrument enshrining the rights of British citizens (currently the monarch's 'subjects'), the Queen's role at the apex of military power is unchallenged. But in a serious political or constitutional crisis, this could have ominous implications.

Facing page. The royal lifestyle induces a value-system unique to Britain which appears deliberately to perpetuate class stereotypes detrimental to the operation of a modern state and a modern economy. The carefully nurtured image of the English country gentleman promotes aspirations and a culture which have no relevance to a country attempting to compete with other nations and to confront its own social crises.

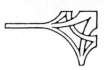

ALL THE
WRONG
VALUES

The rituals and fancy-dress of the Derby reinforce the British notion that success is measured by social acceptance within an unseen club rather than on the basis of merit. The royal mystique encourages Britain's managers to parade in the royal enclosure at the races in the middle of the working week.

Royal Ascot, more than any other event in the social season, underlines the continuing pull of class values in modern Britain. Even if most of the participants only play at being aristocrats for a day, the attraction of the value-system personified by the royals is powerful.

Above. The royal garden party at Buckingham Palace is presented as an informal meeting between monarch and people. Anyone may be plucked from obscurity and given an opportunity to mingle for an afternoon with the royal family. Yet the formality of the occasion and the careful selection of individuals deemed worthy of a royal handshake serve to reinforce the image of monarchy as a distant magical star.

Facing page. The annual 'Royal' regatta at Henley has no direct link with royalty, yet the atmosphere of languid upper-class elegance so self-consciously preserved is yet another by-product of a snobbish and outdated society with the monarch at its apex.

The ultimate sign of having arrived – at least in the mind of the recipient – is the honour bestowed from on high. No state in the developed or the developing world has the vast array of baubles which Britain has at its disposal with which to humour its high achievers. In the 1990s the aspiration to receive an honour from the Palace (as opposed to a material reward or peer group recognition) is an inducement to conformity rather than an incentive to be original.

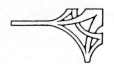

YESTERDAY'S CRISES

Oliver Cromwell's attempt to create a republic in the seventeenth century did not take hold because it came too soon in the historical development of a country whose middle class had not yet fully evolved. It was also too dependent on the personality of Cromwell, whose death in 1658 spelled the end of an experiment.

Tom Paine, Britain's great republican thinker of the late eighteenth century, was frustrated by ruthless deployment of the government's political resources to prevent opposition to the monarchy.

Charles Dilke, who led the republican campaign of the 1870s, stirred up public debate about the heavy financial demands of the reclusive Queen Victoria. Her return to a pageant-ridden centre-stage at the urging of advisors dissipated the republican movement.

The introverted Edward VIII felt uncomfortable under the pomp and the cold grandeur which his father, George V, had encouraged. The departure of this casualty of the Windsor system rocked the monarchy, but only briefly.

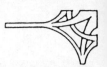

TODAY'S CRISIS

The marriage of Charles and Diana symbolised continuity in the British monarchy.
The fairy-tale nature of the union – of a virginal princess and an eligible prince –
cemented loyalty to the throne, for a time at least.

Left. If the marriage of Charles and Diana strengthened the monarchy, the squalid disharmony between them inevitably weakened it. *Below.* The public relations tool created by the monarchy can also be used against it. When Diana posed as the troubled, solitary princess before the Taj Mahal, the world's greatest monument to royal love, press and public were quick to read her message: her marriage was over. And with it tumbled the prospects of the British monarchy surviving into the twenty-first century.

Like an omen, the fire at Windsor Castle in 1992 cast a pall of gloom over the fortunes of the royal family. Instead of a spontaneous outpouring of sympathy, the monarchy was faced with a tetchy press and a public scornful of the unseemly speed with which the financial responsibility for repairs to the castle was side-stepped by the Windsors.

DAILY Mirror

Friday, February 12, 1993 — NEWSPAPER FOR THE NINETIES — January daily sale (est): 3,454,213 (INCORPORATING THE DAILY RECORD) — 27p

WHY JACKO'S ALL WHITE NOW!
CENTRE PAGES

Necklace victim Stacey's mother is held

By RAMSAY SMITH

THE mother of strangled Stacey Queripel, seven, was arrested by murder squad detectives yesterday.

Gilliane Queripel, 33, was being quizzed about the moments leading to her daughter's death.

Stacey's body was found three weeks ago in undergrowth outside an arts centre at Bracknell, Berks.

Police believed at first that her death was an accident.

They thought she was strangled when her plastic necklace caught on a bush.

The girl's mother raised the alarm about her disappearance.

She claimed Stacey sneaked out of her council

VICTIM: Stacey

flat 400 yards away after being sent to bed.

Neighbours and friends joined a huge police search for the tragic youngster.

Police later grew suspicious about the cause of death and a murder hunt was launched following a second post-mortem.

A spokesman for the Thames Valley force said last night: "A 33-year-old local woman has been arrested in connection with Stacey's murder."

Gilliane has never lived with Stacey's father, Steven Norton.

H.M. THE TAX DODGER

THE Queen is set to become Britain's biggest tax "dodger" – paying as little as £2 million on her vast fortune.

And Prince Charles will get away with a tax bill of less than £1 million.

Details of the amazing new tax deal were officially announced yesterday – after they were revealed exclusively in the Daily

By ALASTAIR CAMPBELL, Political Editor

Mirror. They sparked immediate protests from MPs who complained that so many royal perks will escape tax.

The Queen will become the only taxpayer with a special exemption enabling her to

● Turn to Page 2

It had come to this – the once-revered Elizabeth II was mocked and vilified with abandon. The monarchy so dependent on public respect could not sustain itself once light was let in on the magic.

Destined for a final journey?

in a democratic country takes part in a ceremony which is purposely shielded from the public gaze. Of course, this private aspect of the ceremony is quite in keeping with the workings of a royal-state in which the people have no role, no oaths taken in their name, possess no central function, and constitutionally are essentially walk-ons and extras. In the words of the ceremony they are to be 'ruled over' and 'governed'.

This exclusion of the people is nicely symbolic of the constitutional exclusions inherent in monarchy, which maintains at the heart of the system an act of discrimination that is breathtaking in its scope: the prevention of *all* Britons born outside one family from becoming head of state. As David Lloyd George put it, attacking the blunt and blatant feudal exclusion inherent in the role of the House of Lords: 'Who made ten thousand owners of the soil, and the rest of us trespassers in the land of our birth?'[11]

It is the 'unwritten' character of the royal-state that serves most effectively to exclude the people of Britain from their own government. The lack of rights over information held by the state is particularly alarming when it comes to the public records of the nation, and thus its history, and contrasts strongly with the regime of disclosure in the United States. The historian John Keegan compares this openness with the royal-state's obsession with secrecy:

> America is an open society in the largest sense. Its elites do not treat public life as an extension of the prefects' room or the club committee. And they do so because the nature of American democracy encourages a fullness of disclosure which still causes visible agony to their equivalents in Whitehall ... Britain has never been a strong country in the way that America is today, and secrecy is one of its understandable defences.[12]

The apotheosis of English social exclusivity is the idea of royalty. Yet the term 'royal' is enigmatic, and difficult to define (except, of course, in the prosaic sense of being a member of the family that is called royal). Historically, of course, there was a heavenly link. Under the injunction of the superstition of 'the divine right of kings', royal persons had an exceptional relationship with the Almighty. And, astonishingly, it was only a few decades ago that a large number of British people actually believed that the monarch was descended from God. Professor Michael Billig, in his survey of British popular attitudes towards the royal family, has attempted to get to grips with what some modern people mean when they use the term 'royal'. Thankfully, according to Billig, few continue to believe in royal divinity: 'When the topic was raised, it could be seen that the mysterious quality of royalness had descended from heaven to take up a bodily existence.'[13] However, he suggests that among his respondents 'there was talk of blood, and in this a quiet but insistent whisper of racial nationalism could be heard'. This idea of 'a royalness of blood . . . to be transmitted across history and into the future' contains, according to Billig, 'A notion of the "pure English" . . . It was a whisper, or susurration, of race.'[14]

This aspect of the definition of royalty is certainly no longer in the ascendant, not even among the most ardent monarchists. But blood (and blood-lines) cannot be separated from heredity, and Billig argues that 'what is taken for granted in "royalness" is an acceptance of hereditary privilege . . . royalness, as something handed down from generation to generation, cannot be earned'.[15] Thus, what remains in the meaning and usage of the term is an acceptance of the validity of hereditary privilege. To be royal is to be different: not, now at least, because of special access to God, or because of a distinctively superior blood type which makes the royal the most perfect representative of the race; but rather because of some indefinable characteristic which demands special social and constitutional privileges based upon a 'special' family background. For instance, one of Billig's respondents, although uppity enough to believe that George VI was 'unsuited' for his 'job' because of his speech defect, nonetheless 'did not, for a moment, pause to suggest that he should not have filled the job vacancy'.[16]

Professor Billig's work was carried out before the taboo on monarchy was broken in Britain, and a new analysis of the way

90

Britons dream and think about royalty may reveal different – less deferential – answers. What *is* certain is that a public which continues to accept the idea of royalty as a serious modern social category (as opposed to a simple description of people who belong to a family whose immediate descendants happened to have been kings and queens) will have real problems in adjusting to the modern world.

The question remains: does any of this matter? Is Britain's attachment to an antiquated, feudally derived class system simply a cute, colourful irrelevance? Or can it be seen as a major contributory factor to Britain's decline?

Of course, little in this complex and subtle area is ever provable, however much we may point to the monarchical culture's disdain for trade and commerce and a class-based 'officers and men' approach to management that leads to a bitter and 'bolshie' workforce. Yet perhaps the most deleterious aspect of Britain's peculiar class system has been the weakness of its twentieth-century middle class. The 'gentrification' of business and talent is, arguably, modern Britain's single most intractable problem. It helps explain why the country's middle class is such a tender plant – on the one hand fearful of being thought proletarian, on the other anxious to aspire to an aristocratic lifestyle. And it helps us to understand why we have not been able – unlike the Americans, the Germans and the French – to create a self-confident and assertive 'bourgeoisie'.

It would be surprising if nostalgia for the amateurish and leisured lifestyle of the 'gentleman' had no economic consequences, or if a society in which 'easy money' (from inheritance and property) has social status through royal sanction, and 'hard money' (from work and creativity) does not, were not to create – even in this most Protestant of nations – an 'anti-work ethic'. Similarly, when vocational training, science, technology and engineering are allocated such a lowly status compared to the more socially acceptable artistic and cultural pursuits of a 'gentleman', there is likely to be a certain drag on the GNP.

The existence of a middle class preoccupied with improving

their social position by adopting the values of the landed culture has in its turn created a huge British industrial proletariat which is largely excluded, not only from land and property, but, more crucially, from access to serious education; inevitably, there has developed within it a stratum which appears – uniquely within the Western world – as culture-less, lacking in civilisation, almost primitive. This primitivism displays itself today in the penchant for hooliganism, in the country's anarchic streak, in an almost revelling approach to the nation's lack of education and skills (at all levels), and, at times, in the obvious attraction to war. The bravura and swaggering unleashed by the Falklands War of 1982 was a case in point.

Few now believe what used to be a general public view: that somehow the possession of a royal family sets exemplary standards of living which, in a sense, 'civilise' the broader society, and particularly the 'working class'. Increasingly, Europeanisation is being invested with fulfilling this particular function. The writer Richard North believes that, as Britain becomes more immersed in the European union:

> the safety valves of our previous, and preferred, anarchy are being blocked up, and concreted over. We are within an inch of realising that civilisation is necessary. Although it is a sublimation of the primitive, we have too little left of the old, deliciously vigorous world which once made up our reality.[17]

The modern world is indeed crowding in on Britain's ancient class system. Mass travel and global communications are internationalising (and modernising) our culture. And satellite television is bringing more modern and egalitarian images right into the homes of the British. Over time, this will finally erode some of the most backward features of the British class problem. The middle-class love affair with land and aristocracy will wane as the real commercial bourgeois values of confident 'foreign' middle classes come to be appreciated. And as deference continues to abate, and economic change slowly improves the economic condition of the C1s and C2s (the better-off manual workers), a new, less defensive and insecure 'middle class' will begin – has begun – to take its place in the sun. Perhaps when these trends have fully worked their will, Britain will finally be able to look the rest of the advanced world in the eye, and no longer have to explain away what is, in the truest sense, a *'vice anglais'*.

Britain as royal theme park

British insularity is hardly caused by the fact that the British inhabit a monarchy. However, the idea that 'Britain is best' – and thus in no need of lectures from foreigners, or indeed of any information from abroad – is certainly encouraged by the cult of monarchy. Large sections of the relatively ill-educated persist in the idea that the British are envied. 'I've travelled abroad and people . . . always envy the Brits their royal family,' says one of Michael Billig's respondents. And it is not just the present royal family that counts; royalty represents 'our history', and another respondent offered the view that no other country has 'got the hundreds and hundreds of years to look back on'.[18] It is this kind of sentiment that leads to Britain behaving as though, rather than a member of a changing global community, its place in the modern world is as a repository of history – a royal theme park.

A curious feature of 'modern Britain' is that so much of our literature and scholarship – where genuinely progressive sensibilities might be expected to flourish – is, if not exactly reactionary, then certainly provincial, bounded by the culture of the island home. The novelist and playwright John Mortimer has noticed this literary deficiency:

[We British feel] much as we have always done, near to Europe but not part of it, an eccentric and private island, still listening to John of Gaunt telling us that the Channel is a moat defensive to a house and looking with disquiet and distinct fear of rabies at that ugly hole in the French landscape . . . [19]

Jonathan Israel has picked up the same insular cultural vibes in the scholarship of history. He argues that:

> the deeply ingrained and undiminished segregation of 'British' – in reality English – history from European history, which pervades its teaching and study in our schools and universities, creates a narrowness of vision that has become a powerfully constricting cultural factor. The basic assumption is that everything important in British history can be explained in terms of British causes.[20]

Israel argues that one example of this Brito-centric approach is the distortion of the events of 1688–91, which in his view did not constitute a 'Glorious Revolution' determined by enlightened and progressive persons at home, but was rather a foreign invasion of the country and the establishment by threat of force of a new political regime.

Contemporary British commentary on events abroad which touch Britain is provincial to an embarrassing degree. Some nuggets include a caption underneath a photograph of the US President-Elect Bill Clinton, taken while he was at Oxford University, which claimed: 'In 1968 Clinton exchanged the midwest backwoods for the dreaming spires'[21] – as if Oxford, which in truth is a provincial English town possessed of a good university, were the centre of the world. Even more grating, and archetypal, was the *Sunday Telegraph*'s correspondent who, at the end of a somewhat defensive article on the large number of British journalists in editorial positions in the United States, could write, 'At worst, America might find it has a bit more gossip to deal with; at best it might learn something.'[22]

In this environment, it is hardly surprising that purely British events are still depicted as 'moments in history' (as though what happens in Britain is automatically of global consequence). Alisdair Milne, while director-general of the BBC, was once described in a serious national newspaper as possessing 'the most important job in the world'. This insular disposition tends to become more pronounced the higher up the social ladder one proceeds. 'Ordinary' Britons at least seem *interested* in foreign lifestyles, particularly if they are English-speaking and relatively advanced economically. This helps explain the huge popular audiences for Australian and American soap operas, and the growing interest in foreign sport (particularly American football). Britain's social elite, however, tends to remain militantly 'English': Royal Henley, Wimbledon, the social season and Royal Ascot continue as self-consciously 'English' rituals.

At the very apex of British learning and scholarship, in the university environment of Oxford and Cambridge, where cultural breadth and cosmopolitanism might be expected, provincialism reigns. These ancient universities, although teeming with foreign students, tend (perhaps because of the international invasion) to be inward-looking places where traditional values and customs are studiously protected. Stories abound of the insensitive and unwelcoming treatment meted out to foreigners – witness one commentary by an American student about his time at Oxford, a viewpoint which, intriguingly enough, could also have been held by an 'average Briton':

> For most Americans [Oxford] is a social hell that either leaves you alone or traps you into being someone you are not in order to meet people. The most difficult thing for Americans in Oxford . . . is not how to complete two tutorials a week, but how to meet good, interesting English people and get the 'experience' they came for without compromising themselves.[23]

The provincialism in the culture reflects itself in the politics, and no more so than in the country's relations with the rest of the European Community. An example was the acute burst of insularity which exhibited itself during the fierce economic dispute which dominated British politics in the aftermath of the government's dramatic withdrawal of sterling from the European Exchange Rate Mechanism (ERM) in September 1992. First, there was an almost tangible sense of shock, which affected much of opinion-forming London (as if such a devaluation were somehow unthinkable; secondly, the often frenzied 'post-mortem' debate conducted in the newspapers and on television took place in a context which largely ignored the fact that Britain, as part of the international financial and trading community, was simply unable to construct an independent economic strategy. Thus voices in favour of British 'reflation' (whether by public sector growth, or lower interest rates, or both) argued their case in terms of the need to reduce British unemployment levels – as though an internal domestic reflation (unmatched by reflation abroad, and particularly in continental Europe) would help solve the problem. And 'monetarists' cautioned against such reckless activity, not because it was being contemplated unilaterally, but because of arguments based upon classical economic theory.

What was missing from this rather incestuous analysis was an understanding of the rudimentary truth that the British state, like most other states of its power and size, was no longer able to determine a policy line independent of the European Community, and possibly too of the global economy. This denial dates back to the coronation year of 1953, when the royal-state, apparently staging its celebration of the 'new Elizabethan era', was in reality hiding from the unpleasant reality of a people ill equipped to adapt to, and compete successfully in, the emerging modern world. Put starkly, the culture of the royal-state exhibited a traditionalism (and backwardness) of attitudes and symbolism that had moulded the British into something more akin to a 'white tribe' than a modern nation.

All the country's ancient tribal practices came together and went on show at the coronation ceremony, as figures (in robes and funny hats) out of a feudal pageant – surrounded by the sounds of eerie medieval chanting – played out what appeared to be some form of great and mysterious constitutional witchcraft. The tribe, watching on television, secure in the belief that the past – indeed, the dim and distant past – was sanctifying a new age, could not have known how deadly was this 'continuity' between the present and the past. Instead of representing a colourful bit of fun, the pompous proceedings were laden with hushed and heavy meaning. This meaning, on the verge of one of the most rapidly changing periods in world history, was defined as 'changelessness'. 'Here — look!' the British seemed to be saying to the modern world. 'We still have a Queen!'

The sad truth was that, in the 'modern' Britain which the 'new Elizabethan age' was sustaining, hardly any change was to be welcomed. And today, even in this most dynamic of eras (when reform and flexibility are at a premium), old institutions, and old ways of doing things, are not only too readily accepted, they are staunchly defended. The British grumbled — almost to the point of revolt — about the decimalisation of the currency. And in the country's present great debate about Europe, it is probably best to forget about EMU and the single ecu: it is the retention of the Queen's head on the coins and notes that seemingly remains a fixed point of resistance.

This raw power of tradition appeals to all ages. Britain must be the one country in the world that can produce such a quixotic phenomenon as the 'young fogey' (try explaining that one to a foreigner!). Even our most reform-minded and iconoclastic post-war prime minister (who consciously set out to sweep away the British sense of cynicism and hopelessness) will now go down in the history books for her very British reaction to change: 'No, no, no.' This was Margaret Thatcher's public reaction to the governmental proposals in some of the very early drafts of what was to become the Maastricht treaty.

Britain is leaving the 'new Elizabethan age' with nostalgia resonating in every 'nook and cranny' (to use a phrase out of the European debate) of our national life. The very images we associate with Englishness — kings and queens, castles and cottages, great cathedrals, bowler hats and village cricket — are all drawn from the past, often the very distant past. Our deepest impulses impel us to the arcadian dream of an unchanged countryside. The trappings of our public life are assuming the proportions of a Ruritanian tragi-comedy. Our 'up-market' TV entertainment — *Brideshead Revisited*, *The Jewel in the Crown*, most famously *Upstairs Downstairs* (recently repeated, yet again) — celebrates past images of class. This theme-park attitude to our place in the modern age is deadly and persistent. Our theme for the park is 'past greatness'. Our architects are working away on refinements to the park: in the royal-state, only those anti-modernists who want us to live in buildings of 'cottage proportion', if not exactly to dress up as Beefeaters, are securing the commissions.

Of course, it is alleged that 'museum Britain' (particularly the royal collection) is good for tourism. And in an age of mass travel, perhaps 'selling history' does amount to a sensible strategy for money-making and survival in a very competitive world. A vibrant tourist industry (even one dedicated to 'history') can do little harm – as long, that is, as it isn't taken too seriously. But the British problem is that it is taken all too seriously, to the extent that the past tyrannises us.

It is in the creation of this 'nostalgia industry' that the leading members of the royal-state are most active. In his book *A Vision of England*, an extended survey of his views on architecture, the royal-state's leader-in-waiting, Prince Charles, reveals the full extent of his attraction to reactionary traditionalism. Here his penchant for a 'toy-town' medievalism (in which the whole country is reduced to 'proper proportion' as part of the historical theme park) is exposed. The problem is that this proselytising prince is not only content to advocate his views, he also often gets his way – via a planning process that is not immune to royal blandishments.

Prince Charles's vision of a 'toy-town' architecture is matched by his (and his grandmother's) love of 'toy-town' regiments. The royal family displayed its true colours when, during the early 1990s debate about the appropriateness of Britain's defence posture following the ending of the Cold War, it attempted to overturn the Ministry of Defence's policy of merging some of Britain's 'historic' regiments. The picture on display was archetypal. Here was an attempt to adjust to new defence requirements by creating a sensible slim-line defence policy, obstructed by an eruption of traditionalist *Angst* over the future of threatened regimental badges and paraphernalia. The royal theme appeared to be: 'Never mind the geo-politics of it all (Nato, the new Western European Union (WEU), and that

98

"new world order"); *tradition* is at stake! Never mind the job losses, what about our "historic" regimental spirit?'

Royal forays into the debate about modernity and culture are, in themselves, essentially trivial. Yet they represent a serious body of opinion that is advanced through a network of supportive institutions (in the public schools, their imitators in the old grammar schools, the universities of Oxford, Cambridge and London and their adherents in the 'provinces', the BBC and its cultural outposts in the commercial sector). These cultural guardians of tradition are thus given some kind of 'official' sanction – a very important weapon in contemporary British debate.

The problem presented by the royal-state's emphasis upon tradition is that a society which constantly evokes the values of the past will ultimately fail. This limited 'Vision of England' – existing in a commercial, competitive world – will simply serve to hand on to its children, as part of the much-proclaimed traditional value of continuity, an inheritance of poverty.

6·Fantasy Land: Illusions and Myths

T here is a sense in which Britain's twentieth-century obsession with monarchy and royalty can fairly be described, in the words of the *Independent*, as 'a case of national madness'.[1] Some have explained (and excused) this 'national madness' by referring to what many of its inhabitants see as an unpleasant environment. Matthew Parris suggests that, because the United Kingdom is 'a cold, wet, foggy and unkind country', the British lead fantasy lives. Thus, 'Princes and princesses are there as cinema screens upon which the nation projects its favourite pretences: they are there to act as symbols.'[2]

The truth may, however, lie, not at the feet of the cold, the wet and the fog, but rather at the level of social and psychological development and of the toll taken upon Britons by decades of paternalism. Put starkly, it would appear that too many British people live in a kind of childlike 'fantasy-land'. Anthony Sampson has argued, apparently with conviction, that Britain's 'whole sense of security' rests upon its continuing to have a monarchy,[3] while the psychiatrist Anthony Clare has suggested that 'there's an element in which the British public is infantilised by [the] idealistic portrayal of the Royal Family . . . and this fetish . . . makes people positively anxious when you start to suggest that it might have to be fundamentally altered'.[4]

The 'national madness' about monarchy may, though, be only part of a broader malaise which makes it difficult for large numbers of Britons to adjust to the changing circumstances of the real world. The main symptom of this malaise is a tendency to delusions involving 'expectations' – inordinate expectations, expectations more suited to the inhabitants of a wealthier country than is spelt by a GDP (in 1992) below that of Italy and just ahead of Spain. For instance, Britain's educational and skills level is – certainly by European standards – relatively low, yet we retain inordinate expectations about the country's economic performance, which we appear to believe *ought* to be approaching the levels of Japan or Germany. Also, given the nature of the economy, there is an unrealistically high level of expectation about the ability of the sorely stretched National Health Service to deliver. The assumption remains that the country can afford a quality service, even though changing demographic patterns are causing increasing demand, and technological change is resulting in rising costs. These expectations about the NHS only mirror a more general expectation about the welfare state: a belief that our economy can sustain a universal welfare system without a system of targeting.

For the source of this yawning chasm between performance and expectation we must look to the dichotomy between our real, everyday life and the self-important propaganda of the royal-state. Britain bangs the drum of a British exceptionalism that seems incredible in the midst of national decline. Presumably the feeling is that if the proclamations of Britain as 'uniquely civilised' or 'uniquely stable' are repeated often (and loudly) enough, they will be believed. (A nice contemporary example of modern Britain's problem is the sensible decision of the analysts of a new 'democratic audit' of the government of Britain to take into account a factor based on notions of 'exceptionalism' in people's responses to their questions before coming to their conclusions.[5])

It was only to be expected that the clash between Britain's absurdly inflated view of itself and modern reality would play itself out in Britain's relationship with the European Community, particularly over the proposals for further integration. This conflict erupted into the open during the 1991 Maastricht summit. In the face of the seeming confidence of Germany and France (as they set about constructing the new Europe), proclamations of British distinctiveness were probably only to be expected. Yet amid all the routine banter about 'defending our way of life' it would have been difficult to miss another strain of national sentiment – British superiority.

This modern myth no longer rests upon overt ideas of race, or even character, and as we have seen it certainly does not rest on material well-being. Rather, modern notions of English 'greatness' tend to be couched in political – and governmental – terms. For instance, during the European debate one insistent underlying refrain in London-based opinion was the idea of England's (and, by extension, Britain's) 'superior' democracy, its stable 'parliamentary system' (the 'Mother of Parliaments', no less), which, under threat from various shades of 'unstable' continental systems, might at any time disintegrate into 'chaos' or 'despotism'.

In one sense, these assertions about the unique virtues of the structures and culture of the royal-state as compared to modern European counterparts were rather sad. British opinion seemed to be modelled upon a 'fading actress' routine, for the truth behind all the 'best in the world' parliamentary bravura was that the British were talking up the country's *past*, not its present, relying upon the 'way we were' rather than the way we are. And surely there is something rather pathetic about those supporters of 'parliamentary sovereignty' who lecture others about superior democratic standards, while supporting the one system in the Western world which retains a hereditary element within its legislature, no formal rights of citizenship, and a 'Mother of Parliaments' which, in reality, has handed over power to an over-mighty executive.

Pathos slid into madness as the trumpeted messages emerged about the undermining of British justice (like the BBC, the 'best in the world') by Europe and its foreign judges. The late-twentieth-century condition of British justice – in particular the inability of the courts to protect human rights against the power of the state, and, in the criminal area, the seemingly endless parade of innocent people who have been convicted and punished – was not at issue. (The recent judicial ability to find the innocent guilty of murder has become so prevalent that it seems almost providential that Britain abandoned the death penalty some years ago.) What excited the opposition to European courts was not questions about standards of justice, but rather the fact that they were foreign. Those Tory MPs who, during the negotiations leading to Maastricht, defended 'our way of life' also exemplified the British suspicion of foreign judges by denouncing the European Court of Human Rights for finding the British government guilty of censorship in the *Spycatcher* affair – not because of the opinion they expressed, but rather because they were 'interfering'.

Of course, it was hardly likely that deeply held convictions about the superiority of British (or, rather, English) governance would wilt merely as a result of mounting evidence of its serious deficiencies. What was somewhat surprising was the traditional wilful high Tory complacency which continued to infect the post-Thatcher government on matters constitutional. Amid the gathering constitutional debate of the early 1990s, John Major's Tories tended to fall in behind the idea, if not of constitutional superiority, then certainly of the success of British governance. John Patten, who as a Home Office minister was the government's point man on the constitutional issue, produced the only formal statement of the government's attitude to the need for constitutional change: we should, he argued, 'ring for the repair man only when necessary'.

Where Britain may *appear* exceptional is in the fact that, unlike its European partners, its primary governmental institutions are unbroken, and thus are still redolent of times past. But this is really only another way of saying that in Britain, even on the eve of an historic European adventure, imperial sentiments die hard. Some of the stridency may have mellowed, but forty years or so after the demise of the League of Empire Loyalists, and the day after the Maastricht treaty was ratified by the French in a referendum, John Mortimer, no doubt speaking for large numbers within his generation, could argue that 'it's impossible to rewrite history', but that 'in our hearts we know that we should long ago have formed trade alliances with what was once our Empire instead of ignoring India and taking no further interest in Canada and Australia'.[6]

Contemporary Britain's imperial sensibility may, on the face of it, be difficult to explain. Yet just as the country's institutions possess the feel of unbroken historical development, so too does the Empire. Where has there been a real break with the idea of Empire? The Queen, on behalf of the nation, has headed no formal public ceremony winding it down, nor has there been any formal declaration of apology, or even regret, from the British government. Imperial symbolisms still stand: from the monarchy itself, through to the 'Imperial' College of Science and Technology in Kensington and the 'Imperial' Chemical Industries (ICI). And there are still all too many Khyber Avenues and Imperial Ways dotted about the place.

Stephen Howe has suggested that, 'on any long term view the dominant fact about post-war Britain is surely the loss of Empire', and that, 'the smallness of the space allocated to Empire and decolonisation in almost all British scholarship from the 1940s to the 1990s is, in retrospect, quite astonishing'.[7] Yet is it? Perhaps the British have not properly understood – and internalised the knowledge – that it has gone.

Both the monarchy, with its lavish imperial paraphernalia and ceremonial, and, more wilfully, the 'Commonwealth of Nations' serve to give the impression that the British Empire, although reduced, is still a factor in the contemporary life of the nation. One observer pointed out that:

The conventional explanation of Britain's (or, better, England's) turning away from the world into narcissistic reverie, or exhibitionist violence, is still summed up most conveniently in Dean Acheson's aphorism: we have lost an empire but failed to find an alternative role. Not Europe, not a civilised and quietist insularity, not a rediscovery of nationhood in Britain's historical diversity. One escape route from this dilemma is to insist that we still have a kind of Empire – the Commonwealth of nations which continue to look up to us even if they are abominably rude much of the time.[8]

Contemporary imperial sensibility, although jolted by Britain's humiliation in 1956 during the Suez affair, was given an unlikely shot in the arm twenty-six years later by the successful prosecution of the Falklands campaign (even though the operation in the South Atlantic could not have been carried out without American help). And some of the same sentiments of the rightness of 'British dominion' could be glimpsed again in the response of some of Britain's commentators to the country's role in the Gulf War (even though British troops represented only 2 per cent of the international contingent).

There is, of course, a growing awareness that Britain is not what it used to be, that the country, although still 'the best in the world', might not be as affluent as its neighbours and allies. Yet this realisation often leads to a somewhat defensive affirmation of Britain and its institutions – particularly of the monarchy. Michael Billig's research traced how this works, particularly in relation to America. He argues that:

> Monarchy has become a topic in which the ambivalence of the relationship with America can be expressed. American envy is desired, as is suggested by the leaping generalisation, which takes handfuls of tourists as evidence of general American jealousy . . . The Americans are richer and more powerful than 'us'. They can buy anything they want ten times over. But they cannot buy that which they are imagined to desire above all else. They cannot buy 'our' monarchy, 'our' history, 'our' nation. They cannot buy 'us'.[9]

Recovering our history

Perhaps the greatest victory of all for the modern world's most professional public relations firm has been the successful strategy of associating this history of Britain, of which we are so proud, with the monarchy. It may be that the British, while not particularly enamoured of the idea of political privilege, have supported the whole lavish structure of monarchy because they view it as representing, indeed embodying, 'our history'. This 'Britishness' of the monarchy is, according to Edgar Wilson, 'a black joke'; on inspection, the representatives of the nation's continuity and history turn out, as we have seen, to be German. (In fact, startling though it may seem, Elizabeth Windsor is the first British sovereign since 1707 to have British blood in her veins, her 'Britishness' being derived from her Scottish mother.[10]) Such essentially trivial contrivances point the way to a larger problem: the more general refocusing of the popular history of the country in line with the 're-invention' of the monarchy. For the lavish monarchy did not stop at large castles, tax-free lifestyles and lavish ceremonials. It also, with the help of its friends, attempted to turn the history of Britain into the history of kings and queens. In the 'Georgian age', and the 'Victorian age', and the 'Edwardian age', and certainly in the 'new Elizabethan age', who sat on the throne, and knelt around it, became as important as the great events and ideas shaping the era.

Strange though it may seem, Britain used to be one of the most progressive of countries, pioneering change and welcoming the future. It was the country that gave birth to the industrial and commercial revolution, taking a leading role in the development of science, and even technology. Now, it is in danger of seeing itself as representing the other side of the 'two cultures' divide − as having been, from Shakespeare on, only good at words. It is this kind of distortion that leads to the representation of the most urban (and suburban) of nations as a rural paradise, an olde England where happy country folk dance round the proverbial maypole. And, of course, politics gets distorted too. The country which produced Magna Carta and pioneered nineteenth-century liberal democracy now *congratulates* itself upon having no written constitution and no enshrined Bill of Rights. And what of the nation's heroes? Does Oliver Cromwell take his true position as 'our chief of men', essentially the founder of Britain's ascent as a scientific and industrial power and as a pioneer of liberal democracy? Or, as Edgar Wilson asks, is it a 'travesty' that 'today so many people should fondly believe that it is the reactionary and philistine family [the Windsors] that represent our best traditions'?[11]

The effect of the culture of monarchy on the country's view of its past goes deeper still. Britain has been one of the most practical of nations, with the most empirical of philosophical traditions – the most secular and, above all, the most rational. Indeed, Britain helped pioneer the Enlightenment, the age of reason and science. Yet we now tend to tell ourselves that the Enlightenment was essentially foreign (principally French). Only lately have revisionists begun to set the record straight. As for the primacy of reason, 'Francis Bacon exemplifies it perfectly,' argues Irving Kristol, who also suggests that 'the Protestant reformation – a British mood if there ever was one – advanced secular ideas by weakening the irrational authority of the Church. Britons have taken the lead in the "modern scientific modes of thinking about natural phenomena".'[12] Thus there is now an increasing understanding that an English Enlightenment predated the French. It was English radicals such as John Toland, Charles Blount and Matthew Tindal, and freethinking republicans – in their opposition to the priestcraft of the Church of England in the late seventeenth century – who developed many of the ideas that were to be taken up by French thinkers such as Voltaire and Diderot.[13] Many of these ideas sprang from the notion that reason as much as religion should be the basis for constructing a just society. Yet they were 'written out of history' by anti-republican writers such as Edmund Burke, who sought to create the myth that England possessed no serious radical tradition and little in the way of a body of thought which appealed, based upon reason, to universal principles.[14]

This attempt to write out of history Britain's singular contribution to the era of science and reason fits in very nicely with the needs of a royal-state built upon the foundations of belief and magic. Walter Bagehot believed that such 'suspecting glances' (in a phrase coined by Burke) were definitely to be discouraged, for, 'so long as the human heart is strong and the human reason weak, Royalty will be strong because it appeals to diffused feeling, and Republics weak because they

107

appeal to the understanding'.[15] Thus republicanism, alongside reason and understanding and, of course, 'abstract theories', loses its roots in England, and therefore becomes un-British. And in the process, the land of Isaac Newton, Charles Darwin and T. E. Huxley is reduced and trivialised into the land of a pomp and ceremony now entirely devalued.

The myth of British power

False notions of superiority and self-importance have con- sequences. Contemporary British history is replete with examples of the triumph of expectations over performance, and of the consequences that follow when Britain's leaders take the 'royal' appellation seriously – as though 'Her Majesty's Government' still wielded the power of the Victorian imperial monarchy.

The hapless Suez adventure of 1956 was, of course, the most striking example of the havoc wrought by a misreading of the realities of the country's power position. Unfortunately, the lessons of Suez were not taken to heart either by the elite or by public opinion. Similar over-inflated attitudes have infused official British thinking for most of the twentieth century, including during the acute phase of comparative decline (from the 1960s onward). Perhaps the very best contemporary example of these attitudes is to be found in the decision in 1990 to enter the ERM (which established a fixed parity between the various currencies of the member states of the Community) at an absurdly and unrealistically high level of the pound sterling to the Deutschmark. Of course, the bubble of self-importance burst when the pound sterling, rather than assuming a dominant position among the Euro-currencies, was withdrawn from the ERM and thus effectively devalued. This fiasco amply illustrates the very real damage caused by clinging to grand imperial ideas, or delusions, of grandeur.

These overblown expectations were, as we have seen, on full view during the European summit at Maastricht in 1991, when the final details of the European union were being decided. For all the leaders present, real negotiating strength lay in the performance of their countries' economies; despite this, large swathes of British opinion (certainly according to the more pompous declarations of politicians and press) seriously believed that, in some strange sense, John Major had a hand of cards stronger than that held by the German Chancellor, Helmut Kohl.

No area of British national life has been so influenced by the pretensions of the royal-state as has foreign policy. Of course, Britain's relationship with other countries was a natural preserve for England's courtier class, because, even in the age of democracy, it was an area from which public opinion had been excluded by the royal-state. The survival of the royal prerogative powers had ensured that the House of Commons would have little say even in most aspects of foreign policy: Britain went to war in September 1939, as it did at Suez in 1956 and in the Falklands in 1982, by what amounts to a royal decree.

Foreign policy – particularly the policy of an imperial state – lent itself to a large royal input. But royal involvement has continued long after the collapse of Empire. Britain's monarch is still privy to all major state decisions and secrets. She has as great an access to any foreign leader as do the Prime Minister and Foreign Secretary. She has the advantage – over her revolving prime ministers and foreign secretaries – of continuity of office. And probably most important of all, she has the ability, through the weekly audiences with the Prime Minister (which Downing Street, even in the early 1990s, still feels it cannot abandon), to influence policy. (Of course, there is no way in which the exact degree of influence of the hereditary monarch upon the decision-making process of a modern democracy can be determined, when the thirty-year rule keeps all Cabinet decisions from the public for at least that period of time.)

Much depends upon the relationship of the monarch to individual prime ministers, and upon the 'deference quotient' of the occupant of 10 Downing Street. However, that there has been a general royal 'predilection' towards certain policies is obvious from the events recorded in the public domain. And it is also fair to speak of foreign policy as being subject to a 'royal lobby' from time to time. Following the early 1980s invasion of Grenada by the Reagan administration, Prime Minister Thatcher initially welcomed the action; it was only after Buckingham Palace intervened (to remind the Prime Minister that the Queen was, in fact, the sovereign of the island) that she condemned the intervention by her American soulmate. The Queen also acts as a general lobbyist of the British government in favour of the interests of 'her' Commonwealth.

The Queen's vision of England's role in the world is, as would be expected, based upon the illusions which cloud the thinking of many of the upper-class folk of her own imperial generation. Alliances (like Nato) that help preserve the independence of the state construct called the United Kingdom with its guarantee of a future role for the House of Windsor, tend to meet with royal approval; on the other hand, 'political integration' (as is now occurring in the European union) expunges the very base of Windsor operations, and thus represents a direct threat – in fact, the greatest threat to the monarchy since the institution was established on the shores of the British Isles.

Preserving the sovereignty of the royal-state has been the central concern, not only of the House of Windsor, but also of the post-Second World War political consensus in Whitehall and Westminster. Thus, for most of the post-war period, there has been little friction between the politicians and their chief diplomat in Buckingham Palace. Yet the task has not been an easy one. Britain, as we have seen, came out of the Second World War in a severely weakened condition, and in the age of the Cold War and the super-powers was increasingly drawn under the protective umbrella of the United States. Yet the Cold War was a boon for Britain, enabling the pretensions of the foreign policy elite (including the royal lobby) to be fulfilled for a little time longer. First, the royal-state, in the early years at least the primary American ally in Europe, could posture as a major world player. Secondly, British 'sovereignty' could be secured by juggling and playing off against each other Churchill's 'three concentric circles' – the Commonwealth, the USA and continental Europe. The end of the Cold War brought this interregnum in Britain's political decline to an abrupt end.

110

In the new geo-strategic environment, America would inevitably restructure its world interests, European unity would become the inevitable response, and the royal-state would have no option but to enter into the kind of 'integrative' political structures represented by a United States of Europe, which would bring an end to its 'sovereign' character.

The dichotomy between Britain as part of the European union and, alternatively, as a global power, has, of course, been resolved by the Treaty of Maastricht, yet many British people (particularly in the country's elite groups) remain deeply ill at ease with this projected future. An alternative involving the United Kingdom as a sovereign state with a world role is mooted, and is strengthened by both the existence and the predilections of the House of Windsor. Thus the royal house remains a focal point for those who continue to see Britain in grandiose terms as a world player, while a forum for such illusions remains in Britain's membership of the Commonwealth of Nations.

Created as a stop-gap to help Britain's imperial class come to terms with no longer playing a dominating role in the world, the Commonwealth has served, however, the exact opposite purpose. Instead of creating the time needed to heal a wounded sense of importance, the Commonwealth, conversely, provided some of our more grandiloquent representatives with a false view of Britain's power and role.

The Commonwealth today performs no serious function that could not be carried out by the United Nations (or a sub-committee thereof), yet Elizabeth Windsor's personal attachment to this ramshackle multinational institution continues to distort British foreign policy. It also places unnecessary burdens upon the Foreign Office and Downing Street – particularly during the annual, anachronistic ritual of the Commonwealth Prime Ministers' Conference. (For instance, in October 1991 the royal-led obsession with the Commonwealth led the country's government to decamp, for a whole week, thousands of miles from home, to Harare in Zimbabwe, thus causing the Prime Minister to take an inordinate amount of time away from the real world of Euro and G7 negotiations.)

Of course, Elizabeth Windsor has an official position in the Commonwealth. She holds the title of 'Head of the Commonwealth', as well as head of the royal-state; and she seems to find no serious contradiction (or 'conflict of interest') in these two roles. Serious contradictions have, however, already arisen, when major divergencies of interest and policy occurred between Britain and other member states of the Commonwealth (as, for instance, during the American invasion of Grenada). There can be little doubt that British policy decisions have been affected by this ungainly, straddling, political position.

7· The Royal-state at Bay?

The republican writer Tom Nairn has suggested that the British sense of national identity is inextricably bound up with monarchy:

> There is no power to see ourselves as others see us, and like anyone else the British look into a mirror to try and get a sense of themselves. In doing so they are luckier but ultimately less fortunate than other peoples: a gilded image is reflected back, made up of sonorous past achievement, enviable stability, and the painted folklore of their Parliament and Monarchy. Though aware that this enchanted glass reflects only a decreasingly useful lie, they have naturally found it difficult to give up. After all, the 'reflection' is really their structure of national identity – what they seem to be is itself an important dimension of what they are.

For Nairn, because the 'painted folklore' is 'the stubborn accretion of a long and (until recently) successful history, short of defeat or revolution, it is unlikely to be discarded'.[1]

There has, in fact, been both a defeat and a revolution, although Britain's defeat was not marked by a 1940-style blitzkrieg, and the revolution saw no crowds in the streets and no storming of a Bastille or a Winter Palace. Rather, the defeat was the precipitate decline of the country in the twentieth century, which by mid-century left Britain dependent upon another power, the United States, for its defence, and by the end of the century below Italy and vying with Spain in economic performance. Historians are beginning to fix a precise time for this defeat, in the years of the Second World War. Correlli Barnett argues that, 'British power had quietly vanished amid the stupendous events of the Second World War, like a ship-of-the-line going down unperceived in the smoke and confusion of battle.'[2] And the revisionist historian John Charmley has suggested that Churchill's 'victory' was in fact a defeat, in that by 1945 'the prime minister's policy of 1940 had, in effect, failed. Far from securing Britain's independence, it had mortgaged it to America.'[3]

And the revolution? Well, there can hardly be a more poignant revolution for a country with such national traditions and pretensions as Britain than the loss of formal sovereignty, first to the Common Market and then to an increasingly integrated Europe.

In fact, as Nairn suggests, the whole royal experience was bound up with national sovereignty, with the reality and power of the nation-state. The 'painted folklore' of monarchy did indeed rest upon the sovereign reality of the nation-state. And in Britain's case the nation-state was a royal-state: the United *Kingdom* of Great Britain and Northern Ireland.

This United Kingdom was born in 1707 out of the union between England and Scotland, and today it embraces both these nations together with the Welsh (who came under the rule of the English Crown in the thirteenth century) and the people of Northern Ireland. (Ireland, although ruled by the English Crown since the twelfth century, was formally united with Britain in 1801; Northern Ireland replaced Ireland in the Union in 1920.) Thus, the head of the United Kingdom is not exclusively English or Scottish or Welsh or Irish, but rather sovereign over the union. Should the United Kingdom dissolve into its constituent parts in the reign of Elizabeth II, she would need to renegotiate her position as head of state with each separate nation. No doubt it was this prospect that led her to make one

114

of her rare excursions into the formal political debate when, during the late 1970s controversy over Scottish independence and devolution, she publicly warned against the break-up of the union.

With the increased clamour of Scottish, Welsh and even Ulster nationalists, the United Kingdom is now entering an era in which the nation-state – as a mechanism for providing services and organising politics and foreign policy – is waning, even possibly dying. The prospect for the British, along with the other peoples of the European union, is to live in a new multi-layered political system, in which the United Kingdom (centred on London) is faced with losing power upwards (to Europe) *and* downwards (to the nations and regions) simultaneously! In this new world the royal-state will lose that most precious of its assets: its control over the British people.

There is nothing the United Kingdom can do to halt this process. Its decline as a political player forms only part of a broader picture: of the erosion of the reality and relevance of the nation-state as an agent in shaping the future. In the new global economy, the conduct of international economic policy – particularly issues like trade agreements in the General Agreement on Tariffs and Trade (GATT) – will best be carried forward by regional, or super-state, groupings. And in Europe, competing as it is with the United States and Japan, no nation-state (not even Germany) can act as a substitute for the European Community. The same factors will apply to the powerful new threats to continental stability. With Russia and Eastern Europe (particularly the Balkans) entered upon a period of potential political and economic trauma, the borders of the new European union will see a host of unsettling developments – the prospects of mass migration, low- and high-intensity military conflicts, terrorist activity, and the like. In such an environment, only a deepened and more integrated Western Europe – in which common policies are adopted – can act as a stabilising force.

The Middle East, too, is likely to remain a powder-keg, either because of the unresolved conflict between Israel and its Arab neighbours, or because of other regional disputes. What is certain is that developments in the Islamic world, arrayed before us from Turkey through to North Africa through to the Indian sub-continent and beyond, on what amounts to Europe's southern border, can only seriously be addressed Europe-wide by a common European policy.

In brief, the increasing difficulty of maintaining traditional nation-state postures in the face of the European diplomatic realities of the 1990s and the twenty-first century will help to erode the *raison d'être* of one of the principal guardians of the nation-state – the British monarchy.

What of Britain's relations with the United States? Since the end of the Second World War Britain has managed to cushion the perceptions and reality of its decline by its heavy reliance upon the Anglo-American 'special relationship'. While America's commitments in Europe were extensive and unquestioned, Britain's reliability as America's partner in a wider alliance could serve to bolster the illusion of British power on the international stage. This apparent power served to reinforce the role of monarchy. After all, a great nation – and a great state – could reasonably be expected to have institutions and hierarchies peculiar to itself – however eccentric they might appear – if it was assumed that these institutions had contributed to that state's sense of greatness. No matter that Britain's self-image was in the gift of Washington. The United States, by continuing to bolster Britain's world position (as part of its European policy during the Cold War), also helped to shore up Britain's imperial institution of monarchy.

The unstated but very real reappraisal of the American role in Europe which is proceeding in Washington is bound to have repercussions in London. Although the United States is likely to remain an important player in the European geo-political scene, and will continue, for the foreseeable future, to station large though significantly declining numbers of troops in Western Europe, America has basically signalled its intention to reorder its international priorities. The United States has, in fact, been over-extended for much of the latter part of the Cold War, and now recognises the reality that it cannot do everything alone. In an era in which it will need to address its still huge budget deficit, it will increasingly look towards a *unified* Europe to share the Western defence burden, however ambivalent about European unity it may be on the trade front.

Thus, what remains of the 'special relationship' between Washington and the royal-state will come to an end. Of course, the leaders of the royal-state were quite successful in their personal diplomacy with American presidents in the 1980s. The Queen and her family had close ties with the Anglo-centric Reagans and with the even more Anglo-centric Bushes (indeed, George Bush, as Vice-President, was Britain's great champion in the Falklands War). These American presidents tended to identify, in the case of the Reagans, with the 'film star' qualities of the royal family and, in the case of the Bushes, with their 'English establishment' culture. Yet times change. The royal-state did relatively well out of the Cold War in that it found something of a role for itself – if not exactly as America's 'client state' in Europe, then certainly as its primary supporter. Britain could thus maintain an illusion of independence (indeed, importance) by playing off the Americans against the Europeans. This era is now over. Romantic memories of the Second World War and Britain's alliance with the United States are rapidly fading. The demographic changes in the United States (particularly the growth of the Hispanic and Asian populations) are likely to make the American political impulse far less Euro-centric, and even less prone to view Britain as in any sense 'special'. Even President Clinton – despite his two years at Oxford – is, as part of the 'successor generation' (successor, that is, to the Second World War generation of President Bush), far less Euro- and Anglo-centric than his predecessor. With the fading of the 'special relationship', another strut will fall from the edifice of the royal-state.

European union and the royal-state

Economic life in the royal-state has historically been a domestic affair. HM Treasury would print the money, determine the level of interest rates and set the economic framework for the subjects of the realm. Economic policy would be very much at the discretion of the governing moods – and intellectual fashion – of a very small group of elite, educated advisers. Of course, international trade mattered, but this elite, through its Empire, controlled the politics of trade.

Now, though, the economic life of Britain's subjects is primarily determined by changes in the global economy. Economic policy and management are increasingly the product of inter-governmental agreements and accommodations – both formal and informal – in organisations like the G7 (Group of Seven leading industrial countries) or GATT. The extent to which smaller nations, like the British, can determine policy (on, say, interest rates or employment levels) is the extent to which they can influence bigger national players in these international forums.

Britain reached the point some time ago – certainly by the 1960s – when actions taken elsewhere (in, say, Bonn, Paris, Washington, Riyadh or Tokyo) affected the lives of its people more profoundly than any purely domestic decision taken in Whitehall or Westminster. In the 1970s, when the Chairman of the Federal Reserve Board in Washington, DC, increased the US prime rate, the consequences were felt in higher unemployment in Liverpool or Birmingham or Manchester. In the 1980s – and certainly in the early 1990s – the decisions of the council of the German central bank, the Bundesbank, were one of the primary determinants of British economic policy. This remained so whether Britain was in or out of the ERM with its fixed-currency system.

For Britain and other medium-sized European nations, an 'independent' or 'unilateral' economic policy which diverges from the broad economic strategies employed by the major international players cannot last for long -- not, that is, if Britain wishes to remain a member of the global trading and financial system. Indeed, even if an independent economic policy were pursued to the point of rupturing relations with the global system, it would not be able to deliver its objectives (presumably higher living standards and reasonable employment levels). The cultural consequences of this full integration into the Western economic system have been, and are, momentous. Further foreign penetration of British industry and markets will bring patterns of work and habits of mind that will further erode the old class system of the royal-state. As Europeans, Americans and Japanese establish themselves in the British market, their management techniques are unlikely to tolerate for long the 'officers and other ranks' mentality, or, more recently, the restrictive practices of the unions, or of tradition. In order to compete, British enterprises will also have to modernise.

Yet more fundamental changes are being forced by the imperatives of the global economy than the weakening of the cultural domination of the peoples of Britain by the royal-state. In Europe, economic interdependence is leading to economic integration. Economic integration can hardly become complete without a single-currency, and a single currency cannot operate properly without a single political authority to manage it. It is this reasoning that leads to the proposition that the single-currency provisions of the Maastricht treaty represent the greatest act of supra-nationalism in Europe's history since the Holy Roman Empire – a supra-national reality in which traditionalist royal-state notions of sovereignty become a sham.

The erosion of the sovereignties of the old nation-states, however, preceded the gathering of ambitious federalists in the small Dutch town of Maastricht in 1991 by some thirty years, 1957 being the crucial date: the year in which the Common Market came into being. As for Britain, it is conceivable that historians may view its original accession to the Common Market in 1973 as the seminal event which destroyed the old sovereignty of the royal-state. After all, by joining the Common Market the political principle of the primacy of European over national law was established.

Alternatively, historians may stake a claim for the Single European Act (1987) which set up the single market – stretching from Dublin to Athens – and which came into full operating force on 1 January 1993. The revolutionary nature of this 'single market' is not often appreciated in Britain, perhaps because it was signed, among others, by that redoubtable anti-federalist defender of the prerogatives of the royal-state, Margaret Thatcher.

By giving constitutional form to the most ambitious commercial integration in history, the Single European Act (SEA) all but obliterated 'the nation' as a trading unit. For instance, in Europe's new single market, national trade surpluses and deficits (the old concept of balance of payments) will retain as much meaning as those of Texas or Connecticut. And the SEA further dramatically eroded national sovereignty, by the rather prosaic method of changing the voting system in the Council of Ministers (the forum for the governments of the Community). Until then, 'majority voting' (operating in the same way as the US Senate or any legislature) was strictly limited; and each nation possessed the right of veto over a wide area of policy. Now, however, it has become the norm on a host of issues for member countries (including the Germans!) to be out-voted and unable to resort to the veto: another precise loss of national sovereignty.

Of course, the single European market does not formally put to rest the sovereign reality of the British state. Not only will the Queen's head remain on the notes and coins of the country, but this symbolism will still mean something, for even within a single trading system (with no internal tariff barriers, and with national balances of payments abolished) the Westminster apparatus can still shape a British economic policy, and thus a separate national environment in which British enterprises are forced to function and compete. Europe's monetary union (the Economic and Monetary Union clauses of the Maastricht treaty), however, is a different matter altogether. Although the British government will probably persist in retaining the Queen's head on one side of the notes and coins in circulation (with the ecu logo on the other side), this time the symbolism of monarchy and sovereignty will have no meaning.

At the very heart of the notion of national sovereignty is the idea that in the modern world only national governments (answerable to a national electorate) can alter the value of the currency – that, in Britain, only the royal-state, through its control of the printing press at the Royal Mint and of interest rates, can either enhance or debauch the currency. As the royal-state's pound sterling is replaced by the new money of the British people, however, real economic power will also transfer from the Treasury and the Bank of England to the new European Central Bank. The mandarins of the British royal-state will have as much purchase upon the economic lives of the British people as does the treasurer of the state of Texas over Texans.

Beyond the shifting location of real economic power, there is the symbolic and psychological dimension of money. Coins and notes (and stamps) are a primary medium of exchange between people. For the British, as for other peoples, the character of the notes and coins themselves (the faces and insignias that appear on them) are a day-by-day reminder of power and authority, of identity and meaning. The money of the British is heavily royalised, the head of the sovereign appearing more than prominently on *all* coins and money notes. The top operators of the royal-state have been keenly aware of this cultural power of the currency, of its ability to help condition loyalty and legitimacy among the people. The sensitive nature of this kind of symbolism was revealed in 1965 when the Post Master General (Tony Benn, then a Labour cabinet minister in the Wilson government) attempted to remove the Queen's head, not from coins and notes, but just from the country's stamps. He was unable to prevail. Buckingham Palace put up a fight to protect the Queen's place on the stamps, and even resisted a reduction in the size of the head.[4] The cultural power of the royal head appearing on a means of mass exchange was recognised long before Elizabeth Windsor, by Queen Victoria. Emily Crawford records that 'what was taken from [Victoria] in power by the Reform Bill was repaid in prestige and with interest by the penny stamp [with her head on it]'.[5]

Of course, the reality is that in contemporary Europe 'national currencies' have all but disappeared except as tokens. Regardless of the desires of British, French and Dutch finance ministers, national politicians are no longer able to fix the values of their currencies (by adjusting the spigot of money printing or by interest-rate policy) according to either their economic circumstances, their electoral cycles, or even their 'vital national interests'. Take, for instance, this new Europeanisation of money from the vantage point of the royal-state. Of course, the British Chancellor of the Exchequer lost all but the most nominal control of interest-rate policy once Britain entered the ERM. In the modern global economy interest rates have a direct and fateful effect upon exchange rates, and thus by fixing exchange rates, interest rates are fixed as well – and fixed according to the dictates and will of the most successful economy, which in Europe's case is the German. Thus the British state became impotent within the ERM – unable to control not only the interest rate, but levels of employment and living standards.

Even outside of the ERM, British economic policy is hardly any more independent. The Westminster government, by no longer fixing its exchange rate, has more short-term flexibility, but it still has to keep an eagle eye on interest rates and monetary policy in the ERM, lest Britain's competitive position slip further behind. In or out of the fixed exchange rate regime, British economic policy, by virtue of the British economy's size, its location, its performance, and its trading pattern, is umbilically tied to the Franco-German monetary zone.

Once the Maastricht economic union provisions take hold, the British state will lose budgetary control as well. Even Stage Two of the Economic and Monetary Union (EMU) process – which will run for a maximum of four years from 1 January 1994, and from which Britain has no opt out – insists upon placing an 'obligation' on member states to fix their budget deficit no higher than 3 per cent of GDP.* And in this second stage of the continent's transition to monetary union, the economic policy of the royal-state will in essence be guided and determined not by the British Treasury but by the 'convergence' procedures of the new Euro union.[6] Intriguingly, the broad economic policy which will govern the nations of the new Euro union is set down publicly

---

* In Article 1 of a Protocol to the Maastricht treaty, the 'High Contracting Parties' have agreed to a provision that commits them to not exceeding 3 per cent for the ratio of 'planned or actual government deficit to gross domestic product at market prices', and not exceeding 60 per cent for the ratio of government debt to GDP at market prices.

and precisely – in binding treaty form – for everyone to read.

The British and European peoples will, at last, inhabit an economic environment that, though not determined in their capital cities by their national elites, will, perhaps because of that fact, provide a stable and understandable framework of policy. By 1999, following this process of 'convergence', and the arrival 'irrevocably' (according to the English text of the Maastricht treaty, in the final paragraph of the section under the title 'Economic and Monetary Union') of the new notes and coins of the ecu, it will be impossible to unpick – and, over time, even seriously to identify – the features and contours of the erstwhile British national economy. For along with the balances of payments, the monetary unit of calculation will have been abolished. Europe will then have become a United States; and, as in the United States, the Euro union will possess its own currency, its own Federal Reserve (the European system of central banks), and its own Treasury, which will be located in the Commission in Brussels. (The Commission will be charged with recommending 'broad guidelines' for European economic policy to the Council, which will act by majority vote.[7]

The Maastricht process, of course, adds a political form to the economic defeat of the royal-state; and for nationalists it rubs salt in the wound. It represents nothing less than the erection of the structures of a new super-nation. Everything is in place, including a brand new constitution. So far-reaching are the political consequences (for old nation-states) of the new union that one American observer has compared the European debate of the early 1990s with the formation of the union of the United States in the late 1780s:

> The similarities between 1992 and 1789 are striking: individual states are loosely bound together but recognise they must forge a stronger union, especially for commerce and security; representatives of the 12 states (Rhode Island did not send a delegate to Philadelphia in 1787) meet and sign a historic document which, if ratified, will create a new union; under the union each state remains sovereign

123

except for those specific powers given to the union, and in those instances the union's authority is supreme; the new document requires ratification by the states; a raging debate ensues that the central issue, sometimes clearly stated but as often not, is local control versus central authority.[8]

The similarities between Maastricht and Philadelphia are not overly fanciful. Then, as now, a constitutional convention took place. In the United States it lasted from February to May 1787; in Europe it was called the 'inter-governmental conference' and took most of the year of 1991. Then, as now, the new constitution (in Europe's case a treaty on union) was sent to the states to ratify (in the American case to thirteen of them, in Europe's to twelve). Then, as now, there was a period of haggling and wrangling (with attitudes struck and postures taken) among the participating states; but nine months later, with the signature of New Hampshire, the American federal union came into being. Then, as now, there was powerful resistance to the new union from within the big states – whether New York (under the anti-federalist, Governor Clinton) would ratify remained doubtful to the end. And then, as now, there were federalist visionaries (like Alexander Hamilton and James Madison) whose politicking and proselytising secured the new union.

Some ask why the enthusiasts for European union sought an American-style federal political dimension. Why not be content with economic and monetary union only? Such a purely economic union would, these critics suggest, have properly represented the new realities of the global economy without attacking cultural identity. And by dropping the politics, it would have gained more public support, and thus have more chance of lasting.

Those who drafted Maastricht, however, like the earlier visionaries of the European ideal, saw the argument exactly the other way round. By insisting (primarily at the prompting of the Germans) upon the creation of *political* structures for a new super-nation, they were taking no risks. Their argument would be that, once the cement of new institutions was in place, there could be no going back.

Whatever the theoretical merits and defects of the various approaches to redefining Europe, the option chosen by Maastricht is that of a powerful new union. Traditionalist opponents of Maastricht who worry about sovereignty, Britain's constitutional arrangements and the position of the monarchy are entirely correct in their assessment of the treaty. The new union invades the royal-state, robbing its institutions, one by one, of their power and legitimacy. The monarchy is reduced to the extent that British independence is reduced, and can find no role in the European union because the new Europe rejects hereditary institutions. Her Majesty's Government – the executive authority of the royal-state – is severely curtailed, not only by losing a whole range of policy functions to the new union, but also, in the Council of Ministers, by the loss of its veto power in key areas. The British Parliament – always relatively weak in the royal-state system – loses even more power, principally because the executive is no longer a purely British affair. And 'Her Majesty's courts' also lose out over a whole range of policy, becoming, in effect, subordinate court systems – again, rather as in the United States, where the state courts defer on final appeal to the Supreme Court in Washington.

As if to round off this new super-state, to give colour to the new union, the Maastricht process creates (almost gratuitously) the new category of union 'citizenship' for the peoples of Britain and Europe.[9] This is the unkindest cut of all for the residuum of royal-state national sensibility. For in the royal-state the people are *subjects* of the Crown, owing their loyalty to a monarch; the idea of people as *citizens* possessed of formulated rights is considered by royal-state enthusiasts as an essentially foreign (indeed a French revolutionary) notion.

In this environment, the powerlessness of Her Majesty's Government – the London-based Whitehall executive arm of the royal-state – will increasingly be revealed. Of course, there will be a seat at the Brussels table of the Council of Ministers for it, and thus it will play a part in the bargaining process. But it can be overruled on economic and monetary policy and has only minimal input into the new policy areas allocated by

Maastricht to the union: transport, competition, commercial policy, social policy, education and training, cultural issues, public health, consumer protection, trans-European networks, industrial policy, policies for 'social cohesion', research and technology, environment, Third World development. Something of an independent flavour may be retained in foreign and security policy, which is to be arrived at 'inter-governmentally', by a process of compromise and bargaining. It is, however, highly unlikely that the post-Maastricht world will witness another Falklands exercise, or any other spectacular assertion of independent British action (outside the UN, NATO or the European union). It is not only the reduction in British defence spending which will rule out a major independent military action, but also the politics of the new European union.

This new military reality also has its cultural consequences. There can be little doubt that British military action to protect British interests always dramatically increases nationalist sentiment, which in turn reinforces popular support for the institutions of the *ancien régime*, particularly the monarchy. Such was certainly the case, not only in the two world wars of the century (particularly in the Second World War, after the royal family decided to stay in London through the bombing), but also with such hopelessly misjudged attempts at great power posturing as Suez. The dissipation of nationalist fervour – and hence the lack of a trigger to provoke the emotional loyalties of the public to 'King and Country' – may be seen in the calls that were made, no sooner had they arrived in Bosnia in the winter of 1992–3 for 'our boys' to be returned before they were exposed to serious danger.

Europe and the 'sovereign Parliament'

The position of Westminster – of the royal-state's 'sovereign Parliament' – in the new union will be even more precarious than that of the government, raising serious questions about its relevance in terms of both cost and function. Already neutered in its legislative and investigative function, both by the power of the government and the Party discipline system, under the European union it will become utterly marginalised. Increasingly, law-making power (over more and more policy areas) will pass to the union, and since the union's executive is not responsible to the Westminster Parliament, Westminster can hardly be expected to secure even the minimal powers which would enable it properly to scrutinise and expose the decision-makers. Thus the 'Mother of Parliaments' will be unable to investigate much of the routine *obiter dicta* flowing out of Brussels. Unable to call before it anyone other than members of the British government, who themselves will be merely the 'agents' of a distant federal executive, Westminster will simply lose its centrality in the evolving polity; it will, virtually overnight, cease to be a national legislature, becoming instead more like the old Greater London Council or an American state legislature. (In some respects it will be weaker than either of these models, because the tax-raising powers of Westminster will, in effect, be capped by the union, while the GLC, before rate-capping was introduced, was theoretically free to set whatever local tax level it wished.)

Of course, the Palace of Westminster can be expected to retain a ghostly presence in central London, attracting tourists to the faded glitter and pretension of one of the most impressive monuments to Britain's *ancien régime*. The great imperial buildings of Whitehall – from the Treasury in Great George Street through to Admiralty Arch – will still stand, much as they have throughout a century of national decline. But as power drains from the British royal-state in London, the action that once took place in these buildings will (followed by the lobbyists, the think-tanks and the media attention) move to the various European centres – to the Council, Parliament and Commission in Brussels and Strasburg, to the Court in Strasburg, and to the Central Bank in Frankfurt – which will forge the contours of the new union's economic and political life.

An integral part of the new European federal system will be the European Parliament. And this Parliament – as weak *vis à vis* the union as the 'Mother of Parliaments' is *vis à vis* the royal-state – will increasingly replace Westminster as a forum for debate and a focus of legislative activity. As Strasburg takes over from Westminster, so will European-wide political parties begin to cohere – a process already underway as the British Conservatives align themselves formally with the continental Christian Democracy, the Liberals with Euro-Liberals and Labour with the socialist grouping. (Interestingly, the only British faction which will not be able to align itself with European Party groupings will be the British high Tories, for which there is, of course, no real continental or broader international equivalent. Britain's high Tories, like the other varieties of continental nationalists, will find it hard, should they seek one, to find a home in the union.)

These new loyalties and identities were played out in the early years of the American republic, when the existing state political parties (or factions) took their time in establishing republic-wide political parties. It was only when, say, the state parties of Pennsylvania were able to establish and appreciate a common interest and ideology with their respective state parties elsewhere that the battle for the American republic was won.

As the new European union takes hold, then, in Germany as much as in Britain, political protest will be unable to find expression nationally. The old national structures will be so drained of power that seeking change through them will become futile: to believe that applying pressure at the point of Westminster will 'take back' power on behalf of the British state will be about as fanciful as believing that, in the 1980s, the Liverpool city council could, by challenging the central authorities, create an independent Merseyside. Short of a British national decision to withdraw from the union (a decision ultimately even more economically ruinous and politically traumatic than the creation of the US confederacy in the 1860s), the new institutions of Brussels and Strasburg can only grow stronger, while the *ancien régime* institutions in London grow ever weaker.

There is, of course, the possibility that the magnitude (and seeming abruptness) of the political change from royal-state to engulfment in the European union may create a backlash. The nostalgia industry may get a shot in the arm through a burst of sentimental attachment to old-fashioned nationhood, to a 'lost nation' – particularly should the new union's economic performance falter. After all, the shell of monarchy and sovereignty will remain – functionless, but nonetheless omnipresent as a potential instrument for a revival of the British royal-state.

More serious than any residual loyalty to the royal-state would be its potential as a talisman – not for a 'lost nation' but instead for a 'lost democracy'. Of all the British Euro-sceptic evocations, the most emotionally compelling is the manufactured image of the island democracy held to ransom by a bureaucratic and incipiently tyrannical Europe. There is more than a grain of truth in some Euro-sceptic assertions that the old United Kingdom (imperfect though it was by modern democratic standards) at least provided a veneer of accountability and democratic control.

The old nation-states of Europe do have some kind of record in this area, and were indeed the focus of democratic expression throughout the nineteenth and twentieth centuries. Yet the population size of some of the present European nation-states (not only the royal-state, but France and Germany too) is simply too large to secure real and effective democratic accountability, particularly if, as in the United Kingdom, the state is also highly centralised. Perhaps real democratic control might best be organised through local and regional government, leaving only the larger issues (economic strategy, foreign and defence policy) to the European Parliament – with questions of rights, the citizen's redress against the state, best protected by a European court.

After all, the British royal-state's democratic record is not over impressive. Its focus for democratic accountability (the Westminster Parliament) has established an executive based upon less than 43 per cent of the vote. Parliament has few investigative powers, and is probably the most powerful and secretive executive agency in the whole of the European Community – to the point where political opposition is now increasingly located in the press and media. The truth is that the so-called 'lost democracy' is more myth than reality, as will become evident when the habits of democracy in the new Europe take hold (in the localities, the regions, the nations and the Euro-Parliament). There is little question that it will be the national parliaments, in Bonn, Paris, London, Rome, that will feel most threatened by Europe's new union. Maastricht ushered in a quantum leap in the Euro Parliament's powers by bringing it into the 'co-decision-making' process, and giving it the vital power of veto (and amendment) over legislation.[10] And as Europe's political parties begin to cohere they will inevitably demand for the union's Parliament an even greater role – one which will act as a continuing and automatic challenge to the legitimacies of the national parliaments. In Britain's case, the notion of 'Queen in Parliament' will gradually come to mean 'Queen in a diminished British Parliament subservient to the ever closer union'. What the value of even a ceremonial role will be for a monarchy lending its imprimatur to a regional assembly is difficult to gauge.

New loyalties

In a letter to *The Times* on 2 December 1991, Captain Peter Kim broke what had been a deafening silence on an intriguing constitutional question. 'I have yet to read or hear', he suggested, 'a single word about how the discussions [in Maastricht] will affect the personal position of Her Majesty and the relationship between the Queen and her peoples.'

Leaving aside the issue of whether the British people – or indeed any other people – are 'hers', how right Captain Kim was: this potentially most crucial of issues did indeed go largely without comment in the great British Euro-debate. Margaret Thatcher had given 'the monarchy question' an outing when, after the 1990 European Council summit in Dublin, she asked, rather cutely, what would happen to 'our own dear Queen' in the event of European political union – a point she continued to raise, although mainly in think-tank meetings abroad. Yet apart from these alarums, for most politicians and commentators the subject of the extent to which Europe constrained, limited, or even effectively constitutionally abolished, the Queen, remained a no-go area.

The contemporary British disposition to sweep unpleasant issues under the carpet, to obscure rather than confront awkward truths, was encouraged by pro-Maastricht politicians, who adopted the traditional paternalist impulse that the more emotive questions at the heart of the new Europe were so terrifying that it would be best not to bother 'the children' by raising them. The aim was to dump the royal-state without an overt public decision.

Yet national sovereignty could not be abandoned without also abandoning the sovereign. A new nation-state (federal or otherwise) could not be created without creating a new head of state. And as the major countries of the new European union are all republics, and the new structures of Europe provide no place for hereditary office-holders, there could be no question of the hereditary monarchs of Europe (even on a rotating basis) assuming any official role in the union, let alone becoming President of the European Council. In the new union the monarchs would not possess even an honorific title.

There was also the lurking issue of loyalty to contend with. The British royal-state not only demands that its subjects obey its laws, but also that they be 'loyal' to it. To enforce this sense of loyalty, the royal-state drew up laws of treason and sedition, some of which still remain on its musty statute books, a formal aspect of loyalty that reaches into the armed forces, where military officers still take a personal pledge to the Queen. This 'loyalty oath', which binds the oath-taker to 'defend Her Majesty (in person, Crown and dignity) against all enemies', is, by Western democratic standards, highly unusual, and potentially dangerous, for it amounts to a pledge to a person, and not, as democratic practice elsewhere has it, to a constitution. In Britain's royal-state – where the constitution is both unwritten and unknowable – the armed forces can hardly be expected to pledge loyalty to thin air, yet it is surprising that at no time during Britain's long constitutional development since the Civil War has an oath to Parliament been required from the armed forces.

A formal oath by military men and women to an individual person is a highly dubious practice. When Adolf Hitler wished to secure total control over the German state he moved to change the loyalty oath from one to the constitution to a personal pledge to 'the Führer'. In Britain the personal nature of the oath is sometimes defended on the grounds that it provides a focus of loyalty for the armed forces, who otherwise would take on a more political colouring, giving rise to fears of a one-party state. Yet this continuing monarchical link to the armed forces raises the huge issue of military accountability in a democratic society. Can, in fact, unelected persons issue orders to the armed forces, particularly when they act 'in aid of the civil power'? If there should be a serious disagreement between the elected government and Parliament on the one hand, and the Crown or monarch on the other, whose sway over the armed forces would prevail? Do some officers still see the monarchy as a court of last resort? That such questions can still seriously be asked in a modern society is disturbing.

The idea of civilian loyalty is also highly personalised. In Britain's royal-state the idea of a citizen owing loyalty to a country and a constitution has never taken hold; instead, the 'subject' owes 'loyalty' (or 'fealty') to the Crown, and thus *personally* to the Crown's human face, the sitting monarch. Up and down the country social occasions sometimes still include a short ceremony called the 'Loyal Toast', offered to the person of the Queen herself, while the somewhat grating popular term 'lousy but loyal' refers to working-class loyalty not to nation, country, or even state, but to the monarch.

In contemporary usage, political loyalty has become a slippery term. Unlike the medieval knight or the First World War soldier, few modern Britons would any longer be loyal enough to lay down their life for their sovereign; nor, it would be reasonable to expect, would they even be loyal enough voluntarily to fund the Queen. To be loyal to a country now means little more than an implied contract between the individual and the state, involving a citizen's obligation to abide by the laws and work within the rules of the polity in return for services and protection.

132

Whatever loyalty still accrues to the British state (and, through it, to the monarchy) is being systematically squeezed: between an increasingly self-regarding population whose patriotism, to the extent that it exists, exhibits itself in fond memories rather than sacrifice, and the European union.

In strictly legal terms, the ratification of the Maastricht treaty transferred the loyalties of the British people from the British state into a kind of dual or shared loyalty to the United Kingdom of Great Britain and Northern Ireland on the one hand, and to the European union on the other. Americans understand this idea of dual loyalty, for in the United States the American citizen owes obligations (and, more to the point, taxes) both to the local 'sovereign state' and to the 'feds' in Washington. Of course, for Americans the federal union is the primary obligation, because federal law supersedes state law; similarly, as the European federal union cements and coheres, Europeans too will increasingly owe the ultimate political 'loyalty' to the centre.

Thus the new European union, by providing a complex but concrete new political order in which European citizenship is established, has unexpectedly provided the British with a written constitutional document. And as the political scientist Bernard Crick has argued:

> If we had a written federal constitution, then the consti-
> tution itself would be the symbol and focus of loyalty and
> legitimacy. If we had a constitution we could either (say
> I equivocally) democratise and minimise the monarchy
> (which, to some extent, would follow inevitably from the
> ending of the hereditary element in a second chamber) as
> in Holland and Scandinavia, or safely abolish it.[11]

So, in future, being loyal to the Queen will have no serious meaning, nor will the loyal toast or the loyal address. And to the extent to which these formulations are still used, they will amount to little more than mere echoes of former days. In strict constitutional terms, both 'British subject' and 'British soldier' will no longer owe sole, or indeed primary, allegiance to the British Crown, but instead will be a citizen of Europe, able to appeal beyond the national boundary of the royal-state for redress and for political expression in elections to a union Parliament.

The new European dimension, by acting as a potential forcing house for change in the constitutional position of Scotland (and possibly Wales and the English regions too), is also raising the issue of loyalty in the context of a potential break-up of the United Kingdom itself. As long as Scotland maintains itself within the new European union, it can begin to contemplate independence from England with virtual equanimity. (Support for the Scottish National Party has risen since it resisted simple separation and adopted a European policy under the slogan 'An independent Scotland in Europe'.) And should the 1707 union between Scotland and England ever be dissolved, then the whole centralised structure of UK government (including the position of the monarch) could well experience nothing less than a melt-down.

The fragility of the royal-state

Modern British myth has it that monarchies are stable and enduring institutions. Even during the November mini-crisis of 1992, the self-styled 'constitutional expert' Lord St John of Fawsley proclaimed that the monarchy had 'seen off' worse challenges than the one then facing it.[12] *The Economist* echoed this theme:

> the British establishment famously turns disaster to triumph . . . For the grander subjects of the realm, as for its monarch, 1992 may have been *annus horribilis*. Few familiar with their tenacity would bet that 1993 will not be their *annus mirabilis*, in which they emerge changed, but still on top.[13]

The real story is very different. As monarchy has met the modern world it has faced only two options: it has either crumbled (in America, France, Italy, Germany and most of Europe) or adapted by ceding most of its political power (in many of the smaller northern European states). Occasionally it has returned after being abolished – in Spain after Franco – but, again, without an overtly political role. Some of the East European nations flirted with the restoration of monarchy after the collapse of communism, but only as part of a larger recovery of lost national sensibility.

The reason why so many British royalists continue with the myth is that in Britain the monarchy *has* indeed 'endured' – as a lavish, intrusive, and constitutionally crucial institution. Dennis Kavanagh explains this by suggesting that monarchy 'has proved to be a durable institution, notwithstanding – or perhaps because of – the changes in its role'.[14] However, there is minimal achievement in the feat of surviving in one of the world's persistently stable polities, in a prosperous, imperial, evolutionary society without revolutionary upheavals and with an embedded class system which has lasted well into the twentieth century. When the British monarchy was challenged – in the 1640s – it collapsed, spectacularly. And ever since it has made one concession after another, surviving only by a thousand retreats.

The truth is that monarchy is one of the most fragile of the modern systems of government. The American political scientist Samuel Huntingdon comments that:

A monarchy . . . is like a full-rigged sailing ship. It moves swiftly and efficiently. It is beautiful to behold. It responds sharply to the helm. But in troubled waters, when it strikes a rock, its shell is pierced, and it quickly sinks to the bottom. A republic, however, is like a raft: slow, ungainly, impossible to steer, no place from which to control events, and yet endurable and safe. It will not sink, but one's feet are always wet.[15]

These points apply beyond the monarchy to the broader British royal-state. Britain's highly centralised and secretive executive does indeed allow the royal-state to act relatively decisively and swiftly; yet, in troubled times, a monarchical system's lack of democratic legitimacy and mass involvement makes it much more vulnerable than more open systems.

The weakness at the heart of today's British monarchy is the association of one particular family – in perpetuity – with the governance of a modern state. By turning the constitution into a family affair we become inordinately dependent upon the good fortune of that family being sensible, judicious and acceptable. In a monarchy there is no mechanism for replacing (by election or nomination) a monarch, and thus an entire society can become hostage to the character of one particular individual, whose 'term of office' is for life. (Sections of British opinion used to scoff at 'President for Life' Idi Amin Dada of Uganda, yet this brutal African dictator was only copying the idea from Europe's hereditary monarchies.) This problem is compounded by the extension of the link between royal family and state to the established Church. The 'character issue' therefore becomes much more important than in republics, where the separation of Church and state is a matter of constitutional law.

In Britain's royal-state, the head of state is supposed to represent the nation; in doing so, the monarch is 'above politics' in a sense in which an elected president can never be. Yet this very neutrality – above the fray of mere party politics – at least implies that the monarchy should set standards of behaviour. When behaviour falls below expectations, as it is bound to do, the whole institution becomes controversial, and the country endures a constitutional crisis. Such is the nature of monarchy that in the early 1990s the stability of the constitution of the world's premier royal-state rested upon the fragile state of Prince Charles's marriage to Princess Diana, and his erotic fantasies as uttered privately to his mistress, a married woman.

By contrast, the personal behaviour of presidents in a republic are of much less consequence. Presidents normally last for only a few years, need to get themselves re-elected and, as in the case of Richard Nixon in 1974, can be removed from office; a new president can be sworn in by a procedure set down clearly in a constitutional document. In royal-state Britain, the abdication

136

of Edward VIII was a real constitutional trauma which was played out largely in secrecy, with no rules and with a host of very serious problems for the stability of the system had Edward decided to challenge the elected authorities.

Some might sensibly ask why the very stability of our constitution should depend upon the fortunes and values of one particular family. Or, to look at it from another point of view, why any married couple should find themselves – for their lifetime – an integral and official part of government and state. The burden modern monarchy places upon anyone, let alone an obviously unhappy couple, is far too great. Why should we not be able to 'get our feet wet' without 'sinking'?

The major problem is the dichotomy at the heart of monarchy in the modern age. What we are witnessing is one of Britain's most ancient institutions, forged long before the democratic age, attempting to appropriate to itself attributes of modernity. The institution which came into being based upon divine right, and which even at the turn of this century possessed adherents who believed its members were derived from God, now sees itself surviving only in terms of fulfilling 'functions'. In a book written to accompany the BBC television film *Elizabeth R*, the writer Anthony Jay set out a list of these functions of monarchy and how they relate to the modern age. In a remarkably consumerist approach, which does not fit easily with the high Tory notion of the inherent value of monarchy, Jay asks what service Britain's constitutional monarchy provides that other forms of government do not provide, or provide in a different way, and lists a whole host – including 'moral leadership' and acting as a 'model of behaviour'. He suggests that a monarchy can set a 'consistent moral standard' and that it can also set a 'range of examples of acceptable behaviour'. Among the specific characteristics which the modern monarch should exhibit are 'domestic virtue' and 'submission to the law'.[16]

Of course, by these tests the modern House of Windsor fails. The fact that millions of others would too is, unfortunately for the royal family, neither here nor there. The decision of the British monarchy in the 1950s, and their reaffirmation of this decision in every post-war decade, was to become a popular institution. The dangers must have been obvious. Pop star popularity is ephemeral, demanding a consistency of glamour and sparkle that is simply unattainable. Also, popularity in a democratic age imposes democratic demands. As *The Economist* observed in 1987:

> The royal family is caught between two social forces. On the one hand there is the pressure to move with the times ... At the same time another section of society wants the royal family to cleave itself to more traditional values. It is a difficult balance to maintain.[17]

No matter how low the monarchy, and its family, sinks in public esteem, they are ultimately dependent upon the royal-state for their survival. Of course, the House of Windsor will not disappear altogether – nor may the future of the Windsors be as bleak and obscure as Sue Townsend describes in her novel *The Queen and I*, in which they are banished to a Midlands council estate.[18] Depending upon how the transition to a republic is handled, the heirs of Queen Elizabeth may still retain their celebrity status and their private wealth. Indeed, as the living relations of English monarchs they might even assume a public sector function – perhaps under the Department of the Environment or the Tourist Board – and receive public payments for public functions.

8·Letting Go

Sir Ivor Jennings once proffered the unremarkable proposition that 'our democratic advance has been slow because our people have been conservative'.[1] More recently, Professor Peter Hennessey has introduced into the debate about constitutional reform the more intriguing idea that the British people's essentially conservative constitutionalism, and their attachment to traditional 'English' ways (including the institutions of the royal-state of the United Kingdom, the monarchy, Lords and established Church), may be *immutable* – as he put it somewhat ironically, like some kind of inherited 'DNA structure'.[2] Thus, so the argument might run, tampering with this structure is akin to interfering with the very identity and meaning of the peoples of the country.

The idea that there is some kind of unique and unchangeable social or psychological component that amounts to 'Britishness', or even 'Englishness', is, of course, part of the more general notion that the British are in some fundamental and permanent way distinctive and exceptional – that is, not like other peoples. My argument here, however, assumes the opposite: that all peoples are, ultimately, like one another; that there is no such thing as 'immutably distinctive' social or political characteristics; and that, therefore, political change (even, when necessary, fundamental institutional change) needs to reflect changes in values, needs and interests. Thus, rather than explaining the continuing hold of social and political feudalism on the British by reference to the inheritance of blood or genes (as though blood or genes contained a political element), it is more productive to set an explanation in terms of what is genuinely unique about Britain: that is, its recent social and political history.

How did they survive?

By any standards of normal development, Britain's monarchy, and the associated culture of the royal-state, should have withered on the vine (or formally died) during the industrialisation of the nineteenth century. The rapid growth in commerce and the emergence of a serious middle class (making Britain for a time the most 'bourgeois' of nations) was, in the long term, a socially progressive development – even if its immediate by-products of urban slum-life, social dislocation and deprivation blighted the new commercial and industrial centres of Britain. This capitalist burst – by eroding old social hierarchies and destroying aristocratic culture – should have fatally wounded Britain's feudal culture and political carapace. (Sir Charles Dilke was grievously wrong, but not without cause, when he predicted in 1871 that 'the Republic must come, and at the rate at which we are moving, it will come in our generation'.[3] Yet the century which saw the essential success of Chartism, a dramatic extension of the franchise, the emergence of a serious Liberal Party, a major radical faction, even some overt and systematic republican sentiment, also saw, at its close, a reinvigorated royal-state – indeed one which could stare the twentieth century in the face.

Maybe if the great Liberal spirit of the late nineteenth century – that heady middle-class amalgam of free trade, land reform and constitutional change – had endured it might, as it developed, have overturned the royal-state, as it tried to overturn the House of Lords in 1911. And maybe, if the House of Lords had possessed the romantic courage of the 'ditchers' and stood up to Asquith, it would have been abolished then and there, leaving the monarchy isolated, to be picked off during a later battle. There are a lot of other 'maybes', but the fact remains that Britain's feudal political template successfully withstood the social and political changes of the nineteenth century, allowing older notions of medieval fairness and justice to reassert themselves as part of the reaction against Victorian progress.

It was arguably the Empire which saved the monarchy and the royal-state from extinction – for the not insubstantial radicalism of Victorian times happened also to coincide with the apogee of Empire, which gave the monarchy (should it be able successfully to associate itself with it) some clear and understandable rationale for existence. Thus, probably, there was no need of royal tricks (the reinvention of tradition, a played-up strategic royal illness and recovery, as in the case of the Prince of Wales in 1871): as long as the political elite's attachment to Empire was greater than its desire for reform, the monarchy would serve a purpose.

As the monarchy was weathering the radical criticism (and not a little republicanism) of Victorian times, a powerful and seductive new royal myth was being created which was to reset the institution for the coming age of democracy. But these myth-makers could not, even in their wildest dreams, have foreseen how total was to be their triumph.

The myth-makers portrayed the British monarchy as the single source of continuity and stability, without which the British would descend into anarchy and conflict. This extravagant idea echoes down the ages, and even in 1992 a leading royalist could still argue that 'a country that scraps its monarchy breaks links with the past and thereby seriously interferes with the nation's inner clock'.[4] It was as part of this continuity theme that the idea of monarchical neutrality was studiously built up. Walter Bagehot remains the principal architect of this particular edifice in royal myth-making, for this skilful journalist gave nineteenth-century birth to what was to become twentieth-century received wisdom about the proper role of a monarch: to be 'above it all'. 'To state the matter shortly,' asserted Bagehot in the most famous of all his declamations, 'the sovereign has, under a constitutional monarchy such as ours, three rights – the right to be consulted, the right to

141

encourage, the right to warn . . . He would find that his having no others would enable him to use these with singular effect.'[5]

The monarchy, however, could not properly be depicted as neutral or impartial if it became associated in the public mind with one particular class – thus the propaganda of transcendence, in which the monarch and royal family somehow bestride the social scene, neither aristocrats, nor certainly middle class, nor working class, yet, in some remarkable manner, all three. Of course, such an image is ludicrously fake. One leading republican, Edgar Wilson, suggests that there is simply no way that any royal person can be other than what they are, the English branch of the super-rich, because 'their knowledge of, and acquaintance with, the lives of most of their subjects is several removes from the reality'.[6] (So removed, in fact, that the Queen, without batting a royal eyelid, could speak, in the midst of recession with record levels of unemployment and financial insecurity, of her 'annus horribilis'.)

Neutrality and continuity were, however, only part of the story. What the great monarchy-maker saw as the key attribute of the beloved Crown was its institutionalisation of persona. Quite simply, a monarchy, because it was highly personal, was also easily understandable. Bagehot pulled no punches:

> we have whole classes unable to comprehend the idea of constitution – unable to feel the least attachment to impersonal laws. Most do indeed vaguely know that there are some other institutions besides the Queen, and some rules by which she governs. But a vast number like their minds to dwell upon her than upon anything else, and therefore she is inestimable. A republic has only difficult ideas in government; a Constitutional Monarchy has an easy idea too; it has a comprehensible element for the vacant many, as well as complex laws and notions for the inquiring few.[7]

However, there was a problem, for, certainly at the time of the publication of *The English Constitution* (in 1867), the personal image of Victoria was not in good shape. Roy Jenkins sets the scene in 1871:

The Queen, in her tenth year of widowhood, remained almost totally withdrawn from public gaze and ceremonial duty. Much of the greater part of her time was passed in her private residences at Osborne and Balmoral. She visited Windsor occasionally, but Buckingham Palace was untenanted from the beginning of a year to the end. She took no part in the entertaining of foreign visitors, and expended no substantial portion of the vast income she received from public funds upon the performance of State duties.[8]

A decade or so later, the public relations problem was fixed. Victoria had transformed herself from a selfish recluse, and charge on the state, to what amounted to a mythical figure. She, and her politician advisers, managed to sell the monarch as both politically weak (and, of course, neutral) and symbolically strong. Her enormous behind-the-scenes influence on politics was studiously down-played,[9] until, at the end of her reign, Lytton Strachey could suggest that 'the Crown was weaker than at any other time in English history'.[10]

Tom Nairn records the role of the late-Victorian politicians in this particular aspect of myth-making. He reports the role played by Gladstone, Britain's premier Liberal reformer of the age, as well as that of Disraeli, who helped turn Victoria into a mythical figure: the mother of her optimistic and bombastic age, 'the Doyenne of Sovereigns, the Great White Queen, the Shah-in Shah Padshah, the Grandmama of Europe, *Victoria Regina et Imperatrix*'.[11] Both politicians were deeply conscious of the importance to the 'vacant many' – not just at home but all around the globe – of the glitter of ceremony and of public persona. In this respect, particularly, Britain's twentieth-century monarchs (perhaps because for the most part most of them were dull and unremarkable) served the idealised notion of a 'constitutional monarchy' more than adequately. Edward VII wasn't around long enough to cause too much trouble. George V was more problematic, yet, for all his broodiness, was able to project the neutral posture of a relatively dignified head of an increasingly turbulent Empire. Edward VIII broke the mould:

he was the advertisers' nightmare, for he could simply not be sold as the neutral, 'above it all' figure of Bagehotian myth. Yet his brother and successor, George VI, fitted the bill perfectly. This apparently decent, shy, dull, reluctant king rode to monarchy's rescue as though he had been made (in central casting) to order. And the backdrop of war certainly didn't hurt. His daughter, Elizabeth, was also a public relations success. First, there was the frail young wisp image, vulnerable yet touched with majesty. This was good for the coronation and for the early years of 'the new Elizabethan age'. Then the projection became more corporate – that of the young family built in the image of the post-war British middle class: 'solid, honest, suspicious of intellect'.[12] In the cruel terms of Madison Avenue, however, the Queen has not aged well. She has, by and large, stuck to the 'neutrality' brief with some success; yet her later years have witnessed both the fall from grace of her children and the transformation of her own image from innocent youth through conscientious mother to that of a somewhat greedy and wilful grandmother.

Thus the public relations monarchy (created for the needs of Bagehot's 'vacant many') lives and dies by its own criteria. In order to survive, it needs what no family can provide: a regular supply of 'the right people for the job'. Bagehot provided it with a long run, painted it for battle, yet when the lights went on he could only observe from the front row. His own rules for survival dictated that the performance was in the hands of the players themselves.

Bagehot, although the primary impresario, had some help, in the form of the elegant mind of the Vinerian Professor of English Law at Oxford from 1882 to 1909, Albert Venn Dicey. It was Dicey, as we have seen, writing and lecturing some years after Bagehot, who bequeathed to the nation the powerful idea of 'parliamentary sovereignty', which was to serve as the perfect legal, constitutional and 'democratic' cover for the huge centralisation of British power. Thus the royal-state was born: power was concentrated in a tightly knit group of unseparated institutions – monarchy, premiership, senior civil service, Lords, Commons and established Church – all under the umbrella of 'parliamentary sovereignty'. It was 'parliamentary sovereignty' that enabled the creation of the fiction of a 'flexible' constitution and a 'flexible' executive, when, in reality, what was described as 'flexibility' really meant that power could be used swiftly, decisively, and unaccountably. (The myth of flexibility was in full flow in 1940, when A. Berriedale Keith could argue that 'from the complete legal authority of Parliament there flows the flexibility of the constitution'.[13]) And while Dicey himself recognised that 'parliamentary sovereignty' was a legal fiction (that 'Parliament' was far too weak), what became important was the sovereignty aspect, since in Dicey's Britain sovereignty (that is, the concentration of power) was necessary in order to run the highly centralised, unitary state. It was the executive that became sovereign, and it was to remain so for as long as the House of Commons remained ineffectual – right up to the close of the twentieth century.

Dicey's gift to the monarchy was that this great new theory of English governance constructed in his name no longer divorced the king or the queen from this expanding government. By becoming part of something known as 'the Crown', monarchy and government merged into some kind of mystical unity, creating a seemingly all-powerful network of unseparated power, and thus giving the monarchy much more protection than it would otherwise have received.

Phillip Hall has shown how this ability of the monarchy to shelter under the government affected the tax position of the monarch. For during the early part of the nineteenth century, government finance had become organised quite separately from that of the monarch, and thus, argues Hall, 'the rationale for the monarch's tax exemption' had ceased, especially 'as regards purely private investment income'.[14] This left them in an exposed position until the end of Victoria's reign, by which time matters had, as we have seen, been put right.

Having weathered the Victorian age, the more insistent question is how on earth the monarchy managed to see off the threats posed to it by the twentieth century. How, having survived the age of liberalism, could the royal-state also survive the age of developing democracy?

No assessment of the persistence of monarchy into the contemporary age in Britain can be complete without an understanding of how the 'Irish Question' has come to the aid of the House of Windsor. During the late-Victorian period, when the modern monarchy was being forged, the troubles in Ireland helped the English establishment to solidify the existing totems of nationhood, not least the monarchy. (Later, too, Ireland, as a force for dividing radicals and liberals, should not be discounted. And in the post-Second World War period, the 'Irish Republican Army' has given republicanism a bad name among the less discriminating.) Nationalism was also useful to an English political elite none too happy with the democratic age. Dicey himself saw democracy as posing something of a threat to civilisation and liberalism, and national sentiment as the 'only principle which could restrain democracy's excesses'.[15] (It is interesting to note here that, although clever, the English upper-class political impulse of this period was fairly limited: to use nationalism as a weapon against democracy, and not the liberal notion of 'rights' – the much more secure guarantor of the individual against the mob – was not only foolish, but destructive too.)

Thus, when the fires of nationalist sentiment were stoked by the traumas and ravages of two world wars, the monarchy benefited. Decades of skilful association of the royal institution with the national interest paid off, and during the Second World War the decision of the King and royal family to stay put in Buckingham Palace (and 'look the East End in the face') was a masterly public relations move which paid considerable dividends. The photo-opportunities afforded by the war – visits to blitzed sites, the King with 'his' troops before D-Day, the princesses in their military uniforms – all helped to endear the royal personalities to an exhausted and often demoralised population. What might have become a sullen resentment against distant privileged royals was turned by an intelligent use of the wartime psychology into a strong current of affection and respect.

Thus nationalism played its part. Yet perhaps it was the growth of Britain's variant of socialism during the twentieth century that, more than anything else, saved the royal house. There can be little doubt that by far the most important social development in Britain during the twentieth century was the emergence of a powerful trade-union movement, which, despite defeat in the 1926 General Strike, came to dominate the domestic politics of the century: Conservative governments reacted to it, Labour ones were aligned with it. Yet at no point did this 'workers' movement', even during its most militant phases (in the period just before the First World War and in the 1970s and early 1980s), even begin to embrace republican ideas and sentiment. Its 'Labourist' ideology (mixing social conservatism with a determination to work for economic advance through existing industrial structures), reflecting the general views of its members, simply would not countenance bringing the monarchy – or the general structure of government – into the political arena. No more did the socialists, who provided the Labour Party with what passed for its 'radical' dimension! In fact, the allure of socialism served simply to bolster the monarchical state by deflecting the radical spirit of a whole generation away from the reform of government and towards the search for public ownership and economic equality. Socialists were normally not hostile to notions of republicanism; but they tended to see the question of reforming the royal-state (whether monarchy, Lords, Church disestablishment or reform of the House of Commons) as essentially nineteenth-century liberal issues which, though good in themselves, would not help forward their economic agenda. Indeed, even as late as the 1960s and 1970s, it tended to be the intellectuals on the Labour right (and later in the SDP), rather than the socialists on the Labour left, who raised the issues of constitutional reform (although Tony Benn was a primary exception here). It is intriguing to note that the Labour Party's very recent conversion to constitutional reform (replacing the House of Lords and introducing a Bill of Rights) has taken place in an era in which traditional socialism is dead. Indeed, twentieth-century socialists saw a strong state, and a united and collectivist sensibility, as essential for engineering the redistribution of wealth and income which was at the centre of their philosophy. And these essentially top-down and paternalist mechanisms needed for the 'transformation' of society were best enhanced by the continuation of the monarchy and its highly centralised royal-state.

From the perspective of the House of Windsor, a dose of welfare paternalism was no bad thing. Elizabeth Windsor, rather like many a high Tory, has always been keen on the ameliorating effects of the welfare state. This was one of the reasons for her distaste for the ideas behind the creation of an 'enterprise society', which, as well as building up a more individualist and less deferential population, might so destabilise the economic system that it would bring into question the whole hierarchical structure. Thus, for a time, monarchy and socialism, though never really friends, made common cause.

If, ironically, both war and socialism turned out to be conservative forces in twentieth-century British history, then so too, for a time anyway, did the new technology of mass communications. The first major public event brought directly into the homes of millions of people by television was the 1953 coronation. This was 'Britain's longest outside broadcast, lasting seven hours fifteen minutes from 10.15 a.m. until 5.30 p.m. . . . followed by "New Elizabethan Age" panegyrics'.[16] This event – together with other carefully controlled royal television excursions (like the early Christmas broadcasts to the Commonwealth, the Investiture of the Prince of Wales and Richard Cawston's film, *Royal Family*) – boosted the 'star' quality of the institution, and also its legitimacy: in a survey published in *New Society* in 1969 three-fifths of children between eight and twelve thought the Queen was 'the most important person in England'.[17]

Even in the early decades of the television packaging of the royal family, there were serious worries about the long-term effects. The critic Milton Shulman aired one of them in 1969: 'is it . . . wise for the Queen's advisers to set as a precedent this right of the TV camera to act as an image-making apparatus for the Monarchy? Every institution that has so far attempted to use TV to popularise or aggrandise itself has been diminished and trivialised by it.'[18] And Andrew Duncan could ask, 'Was the reality of Monarchy merely a family of ham actors, pre-packed in the flotsam of an imperial past and the jetsam of inherited attitudes, pirouetting in a televised home movie?'[19]

These misgivings apart, everything was all right as long as the new mass communications system remained suitably deferential. And between 1945 and, say, 1990 it did – certainly so in matters to do with the royal family and the vitals of the royal-state constitution. The Reithian ideology of the BBC – that peculiar amalgam of improving public service and reverence for traditional authority and structures – saw to that, using its monopoly power (and then, after the arrival of commercial television, its leading position in the industry and the public's reliance on it for 'official' information) to influence the standards, mores and loyalties of a whole generation. In the nearest that a free and pluralistic society has yet come to totalitarian cultural 'programming', the British people – forced under pain of jail to pay a tax (licence fee) – had fed back to them what amounted to the 'vision' of a small group of primarily public-school-educated males. This vision included the accepted paternalist notion of the time, that the monarchy was a source of stability and example, good for the folk.

Of course, such a 'programming' was possible only because of another feature of the age of paternalism – the generalised low level of mass education. It is instructive (and somewhat sad) to read Christopher Hill arguing that 'I have tried to explain the seventeenth-century [*and not only seventeenth-century*] problem republicans faced with an uneducated electorate, specifically a politically un-educated electorate.'[20] Fantasising about royals, dreaming of the Queen, deferring to 'betters' – all these characteristics of royal-state Britain were unsurprising among a population made up of men and women who had left school before sixteen, having been told that not only rigorous academic standards, but also reflective and critical thought, was not for them.

Identity crisis: the stumbling-blocks of transition

Dean Acheson's hurtful quip that Britain had 'lost an empire and not yet found a role' struck home more than forty years ago; yet it is still relevant today. In the 1990s, the country is still lost in the world – finding itself between roles, between constitutions, and even between nation-states.

It will take a lot for the British to let go of the past and its most evocative symbol – the monarchy. Thus, even with the tides of democratic change at home and geo-political change in Europe running swiftly against the monarchy, there remains a marked reluctance on the part of domestic British public political figures to join in the growing national debate about royalty's future.

Of course, few in the modern British political class can possibly believe some of the sanctimony and syrup they dole out whenever the issue of royalty arises. They cannot possibly believe all the antiquated court guff they have to espouse, and enjoy all the verbal and physical bowing and scraping they have to endure. Yet John Major (with his vision of a 'classless society'), former Labour leader Neil Kinnock (with his erstwhile republican sympathies) and Liberal leader Paddy Ashdown (with his commitment to democratic constitutional change) have all paid obeisance to the monarchy – and in fulsome terms.

There are powerful reasons why our politicians are not yet able openly to support a democratic constitution. Some of them are obvious. Politicians need to get themselves elected, and in their search for votes are loath to alienate any group of electors who might switch to their opponents; they are well aware that an important voting bloc of older folk, who associate the Queen personally with their own lives, would still be offended and shocked by republican sentiments. Politicians are also fearful of being labelled unpatriotic, and this same bloc of older electors tend to believe that Britain and the Queen go together – despite the fact that the House of Windsor is partly German by derivation, and that many of the country's prominent republicans (Tom Paine, John Stuart Mill, Charles Dilke, Joe Chamberlain, William Thackeray, H. G. Wells, not to mention Oliver Cromwell) were nothing if not English. However, some of the reasons for official reticence on the monarchy issue are not so transparent. A goodly number of our elected politicians seek an old age in the House of Lords (what the Tory MP

150

Richard Shepherd described as our national 'sunset home'),
and they are well aware that any move to dismantle the
monarchy would inevitably be preceded by an abolition of the
upper House.

Britain's politicians have historically been gagged by an
unhealthy official parliamentary 'vow of silence' (enforced by
the Speaker), in which criticism of the royal family by the elected
representatives of the people in the 'Mother of Parliaments' was
forbidden. Only very recently, following the Prime Minister's
statement on the separation of the Prince and Princess of Wales
in 1992, when two Labour MPs, Dennis Skinner and Bob Cryer,
made some less-than-complimentary remarks about the royal
institution, has the convention been breached. However, MPs'
questions to the Home Office about many royal matters will
continue to be severely discouraged by the whips.

This brings us to the question of the oath of loyalty to the
Queen taken by, among others, judges and the armed forces.
The various oaths differ somewhat, but all contain the same
pledge of *personal* fealty to the monarch. Some would argue
that, no matter how opinions may subsequently change, all
those who have taken the oath are, in a sense, spoken for, their
loyalties frozen in an earlier act of obeisance. However, others
contend that, as the oath of allegiance for, say, magistrates
insists upon a declaration that the person sworn 'be faithful
and bear true allegiance to Her Majesty Queen Elizabeth II,
her heirs and successors according to law', the oath is to the
head of state, not to the monarch, so that, should Parliament
create a republic, such allegiances would automatically transfer
to a president or, hopefully, a constitution. It is the 'according to
law' wording in the oath which provides the release for those of
a legalistic disposition.

This rigmarole of oath-taking and pledges of loyalty has
created a climate in which, until very recently, criticism of
the monarch was thought of, in some inchoate but real sense,
as 'treasonable'. Jokes are still made – not always wholly
lightheartedly – about republicans 'being sent to the Tower'.
Also present – in a ghostly kind of way – is the law on sedition.
This piece of legal antiquity makes it technically unlawful to

agitate in favour of the overthrow of existing state authorities, including the monarchy (involving 'conduct or speech tending to rebellion or breaches in public order'). As this is precisely what republicans seek to do – by peaceful means – then they may indeed be in breach of the law. Of course, should a prosecution be attempted under the law on sedition, much would turn on the meaning of words; and the whole exercise would fall foul of the modern human rights imperative of peaceable free speech.

The power of these kind of unrepealed 'olde English' laws lies not in prosecutions and convictions made under them, but rather in the nagging, overhanging threat they pose to those who seek real constitutional change. Michael Shrimpton, a supporter of the virtues of the *ancien régime* and a visceral opponent of the European union, used the letters page of *The Times* to make the somewhat menacing assertion that an advocate of republicanism 'might derive some profit from a close reading of the law on sedition'.[21]

On top of these constraints, there is also an understandable and natural *politesse* at work here – that of not wanting to offend the Queen – although perhaps even the most ardent monarchist might appreciate that such concerns should hardly serve as a reason for precluding a great national debate about the nature of the constitution. This reticence is still prevalent, even now, when republicanism has become respectable. One of the intriguing aspects of this great national shyness is the way in which it has also affected constitutional reformers. They too had difficulty in 'letting go'.

Following Britain's last serious bout of thinking about constitutional issues (prodded by the reforming campaign of Richard Crossman and John Macintosh), the awesome-sounding Royal Commission on the Constitution was set up. This brought forth merely a mouse. There was no reference to the need for a written constitution, no suggestion of a Bill of Rights and, naturally, nothing at all about reforming the monarchy. Of course, this Commission was restricted by its complacent and limited terms of reference, which instructed it to work for 'the good government of Our people under the Crown'.[22] Thus, when new draft constitutions – like that of the Labour-inclined Institute for Public Policy Research in autumn 1991 – even though they depth-charged virtually every ship of the constitutional line, they left the monarchy intact. It was the same when the Liberal Democrats entered the fray. Their draft constitution – issued in the form of a Federal Green Paper and entitled 'We, the people' – started with great promise. It argued for a wholesale restructuring based upon the introduction of a written constitution (following a Constituent Assembly), the replacement of the House of Lords by an elected senate and the creation of a Supreme Court.[23] Yet again, the monarchy remained untouched. Even though the Liberal Democrats proclaimed that the hereditary principle in the House of Lords was 'indefensible', they argued for the retention of 'Her Majesty' as part of the institution of Parliament (together with a House of Commons and a Senate). There was, however, a subtle devaluation of the role of monarchy, which was placed firmly within the confines of a written constitution. Also, by proposing that the prime minister should take an American-style oath (to 'defend the constitution of the United Kingdom'), rather than an oath to the monarch, the focus of loyalty was altered. But the head of state of the 'United Kingdom' (the feudal depiction of the nation still, in 1990, preferred by the Liberal Democrats) would remain an hereditary office.

More radical than Labour and the Liberal Democrats (who were both constrained by the exigencies of electoral politics) was the doyen of pressure groups for constitutional change, Charter 88. Yet even this reforming organisation retained the monarchy at the apex of its proposed new constitutional system. It did so by omission. Its original declaration included every conceivable republican nostrum – from disestablishing the Church of England to basing the constitutional structures upon the theoretical underpinning of the 'sovereignty of the people' – yet the historic republican aspiration of creating a presidency for Britain did not feature. In its updated Manchester Declaration (issued after its very successful convention in the autumn of 1991), Charter 88 still omitted any reference to the monarchy. Although the Manchester Declaration stated that 'our basic rights must be entrenched so that we cease to be

153

subjects and become citizens', the institutional reform needed to allow such a transition – the abolition of the monarchy – was not made explicit.

Of course, Charter 88 was founded (in 1988) at an early stage in the constitutional reform era – and it appealed for signatories (and received many thousands) on the basis of a list of ideas which, radical for its time, have nonetheless become somewhat orthodox. By the early 1990s its officers felt that to return to its signatories for a mandate to campaign on the monarchy issue would still be counter-productive; and thus for Charter 88 republicanism remained implicit rather than explicit. Increasingly, however, the signatories of the Charter were making their republican sensibilities heard, and at the time of writing it is probably only a matter of time before the *de facto* republicanism of the organisation becomes the *de jure* position.

The problem posed by the monarchy to the constitutional reform movement was by no means unique to pressure groups. A whole range of pro-change political theorists (even radicals) were, even as late as the early 1990s, still refusing to touch the issue of royalty. For instance, in an edition of *Parliamentary Affairs* specifically concerned with the question of constitutional reform (October 1991), not once was the monarchy referred to as even part of a package of reforming measures. Learned articles on 'Citizenship and the Constitution', 'Europe and Sovereignty', 'Citizenship and Youth', 'On Writing a Constitution' could work their will on the page without any mention at all of Britain's monarchy. Typical of this reticence was the constitutional world-view of Vernon Bogdanor, a Reader in government at the University of Oxford. He was able to disengage the monarchy from the more general constitutional reform programme by arguing that there was no particular connection between the Queen and the House of Lords. This ingenious thesis suggested that, although both institutions were indeed based upon the hereditary principle, the Lords (being an 'active' part of the legislative process) could indeed be abolished whereas the monarchy (being 'inactive') need not be touched.[24]

Of course, Bogdanor is technically correct. The Lords does indeed take part in the legislative process (and can delay, even effectively veto, legislation coming to it from the House of Commons), whereas the runes have it that it is 'inconceivable' that the Queen would veto a legislative proposal. However, we cannot really know about the view of the Queen without asking her. And in Britain's royal-state there is no mechanism for questioning the monarch. She does not hold press conferences. Moreover, there is no likelihood of such an inquiry, at least not from any public official, and any enquiry from an ordinary subject would be referred to the Home Office. Thus 'inconceivable' is not proven. In any event, this approach of the Bogdanor school of thinking rests, as does much constitutional stasis, upon assertion only.

Reticence about raising the issue of monarchy went beyond the constitutional reforming organisations. Anthony Sampson, for example, spoke for many reformers when he argued that, although 'Republicanism is certainly now talked about openly, as it never was over the last thirty years,' there were 'dangers' in a presidency, and (as if the German or Italian or Irish presidencies served no function) 'the greatest service a monarchy can render to a democracy is to separate pomp from power'.[25]

Can we adjust?

The question remains. Can Britain come to terms with the imperatives of a new world – with the twin imperatives of, on the one hand, domestic democratic change, and, on the other, a reduced status within Europe and the global economy? Will we ever be able to set aside the idea of exceptionalism and take in the idea that other countries are at least as stable, at least as democratic, as we are – and in some respects more so? And will we ever seriously believe that foreigners – particularly the more successful ones – may have something from which we can learn?

In one sense the questions answer themselves. Britain will have to adjust, because it has no alternative. In this sense Britain, as it enters the new European age, resembles the American

South in the 1950s. Dixie then, like Britain now, was part of a wider economy from which it could not escape, and its economic and political freedom to manoeuvre was extremely limited. It was also, again like Britain now, having to face profound changes caused by the dissolution of a traditional society. Yet post-war Dixie (again like Britain now) was also proud of its history, consumed with defending its identity and its 'way of life', and strong on old-fashioned ways of doing things. It was also deeply suspicious of abstract 'rights' and of those who attempted to secure a more open society through the civil rights movement. Consequently, there was bitter resentment of 'alien' influence (particularly that of outside judges) and much talk of sovereignty (in this case, the rights of 'sovereign states'). Also like 1950s Dixie, Britain's process of adjustment will be most difficult among traditional elites – those who did well out of the previous system and see their cultural dominance eroded by having to compete for power, influence and resources in their own domestic backyard.

The analogy with the 1950s American South can be stretched further. Dixie's elites, like many in contemporary Britain, did well out of an anti-egalitarian, heredity-based culture in which style and manners counted for much more than bourgeois production and competition. They feared the change which would be wrought by this more commercial culture of the economically dynamic neighbouring states.

Only as recently as a few decades ago, Britain possessed the most formidable and illustrious landowning upper class of modern times. David Cannadine has described the sheer raw power of Britain's aristocracy as it existed in the late nineteenth century: 'In terms of territory, it seems likely that the notables owned a greater proportion of the British Isles than almost any other elite owned of almost any other country.'[26] It seems likely that this pattern has continued into the present time, with wider share ownership in Britain not duplicated by wider land ownership. And this landed interest in Britain, although no longer such a dominant group in terms of raw resources, still acts, by its social influence upon other elites (both commercial and professional), as a conservative and traditional cultural

156

bastion – and, remarkably, unlike any other similar group in the world, still possesses its own tame legislative chamber.

Yet these traditionalist British elites, again like those of Dixie some decades ago, sense that the tide of history is flowing against them, that a new chapter has opened and that there is no alternative but to make their way in a new environment. Although suspicious of democratic and foreign culture, and of federal power centres, there was no question of Dixie seceding from the union.

Of course, the parallel may be somewhat overdrawn. Unlike Dixie, Britain can draw upon a powerful political tradition of liberalism; adjustment to a more democratic age, in which an erstwhile isolated culture will need to merge with others, may therefore be somewhat easier. Yet like the American South, Britain will need to junk its myths about itself (particularly its innate sense of superiority) in order to do it. And in order to successfully complete the adjustment, Britain will need to dismantle institutional hurdles such as the structures of its *ancien régime* royal-state. Its people will need to alter ingrained attitudes. The Thatcher period was supposed to induce a more enterprising culture in which individualism would thrive, yet although the crucial role of the individual may now be somewhat more appreciated in the economic sphere, it is still undervalued in the political and cultural. We still, instinctively, think far too collectively – in its reactionary sense. The modern individual's primary relationship – to 'family and friends' – is still somewhat distorted by generalised, created loyalties to 'Queen and Country' nationhood and old-fashioned classes.

A decline in reactionary collectivism – in the sense that it separates and cuts off and excludes individuals according to group loyalty and identity – will weaken the ties to 'us' and 'them'. This division has less resonance than it used to have, in terms of class. It is, though, still powerful in terms of nation – although in any serious meaning of the term (economically, geo-politically, even culturally), 'us' should now include Spaniards, Italians, Greeks, as well as the Germans, the Dutch and the French.

Loyalties to traditional collectivities (like class and nation), and their symbolic representations (like the monarchy) are irrelevant in the wider economic marketplace, in the global economy and in the political union. Survival in this new environment demands a keen sense of individuality, of the rights and obligations of the individual, and of the relationship of that individual to the state. In other words, it demands the skills of *citizenship*. Low personal aspirations, unassertiveness, social acquiescence, an unquestioning acceptance of where each individual fits in the overall order of things – all these have been the lot of most of the British while under the sway of the culture of Empire and monarchy. They are no longer a guide for living.

9· A Dynamic Union

Our new constitution

The big question in British politics is not whether Britain needs a modern constitution, but rather how to get it. How, in fact, does Britain get from A to B: from one day in which it exists under a royal-state and monarchy with no formal rules, to another day in which it becomes a republic with a written constitution?

This question is still one of the few remaining cards possessed by the traditionalists in the modern constitutional debate. After all, they argue, there is no mechanism for changing an unwritten constitution into a written one, or for replacing the monarchy with a presidency. 'We British', so the traditionalist theme would run, 'simply do not operate this way – we evolve, change by accretion and evolution. To create a republic and a written constitution would be an alien act of revolution.' What is more, the argument would proceed, who is going to write the new republican constitution? Who is going to ratify it? Will there be agreement on the details, let alone the fundamentals, of the new document? Won't the drawing up of a new constitution simply lead to an unseemly wrangle between socialists, liberals, conservatives, as they try to secure special clauses and guarantees? Wouldn't it be more sensible simply to settle for a *reform* of the royal-state and the monarchy?

Actually, in one sense, a new constitution for the British people has already been written, ratified and enacted. For the Maastricht treaty – creating the new European union – not only amounts to a new constitutional document, replacing the legitimacy of the royal-state, but it also opens a whole new constitutional era. Neal Ascherson saw the radical potential in all this when he argued that 'closer union will break it [the 'Westminster machine'] down altogether, forcing the first complete constitutional reform for 300 years. To me, that is the main attraction of Maastricht.'[1]

Ascherson was right. The change in the political life of Britain induced by the new European dimension – and, particularly, the new European union treaty – is the most profound, not just for three hundred, but for over a thousand years. Magna Carta, the civil war in England, the settlement of 1688, and all subsequent reforms and upheavals were all purely domestic affairs, altering the character, but not the main premiss, of the British royal-state. But the political union being born in Europe in this last decade of the twentieth century absorbs the British state into a new and larger political formation. The United Kingdom (like Scotland in 1707 following an earlier union) may retain the symbols of nationhood, but little else.

Maastricht, and the union it creates, possesses all the basic characteristics of a constitution. First, and crucially, it is written. Britain is a country without a written document, and in search of one. This the union treaty, by providing a fundamental framework for rights, laws and the political legitimacy of institutions, provides. And by setting out in essentially the same manner as does the US constitution, or any written constitution, the various powers of different levels of government, it thereby limits them. For instance, by virtue of the new union treaty Britain's institutions (including Parliament and Britain's over-powerful executive branch) are for the very first time finally brought under some kind of constitutional limitation. Institutions that were hitherto unaccountable, limited not by law or constitution but only by 'good sense', history and what the constitutional sages said they could get away with, can now be restrained by constitutional means.

By setting out the powers of, and relationships between, the 'federal' institutions in Brussels and Strasburg on the one hand, and the domestic national institutions in London on the other, the new union creates for the British people, again for the very first time in their history, a federal constitution. Since the early 1960s the politicians of the royal-state have been dithering about Scottish and Welsh self-government and devolution; yet here, in one fell swoop, is a constitutional framework for a federal solution to the 'Scottish', 'Welsh', 'Northern Irish' and 'English' question. In the early years of the new union it will be Britain as a whole that is in a federal relationship to Brussels; but should, say, Scotland secede from the 1707 Act of Union, then presumably it would be free to join the European union possessed of the same rights as any other member state. (The question of whether 'successor states', emerging out of the break-up of a member state of the union, can automatically assume all the rights of a member state is still somewhat cloudy. The British government tends to argue that they would not. The Scottish National Party says that, upon assuming some of the largest oil and fishing rights in the European union, the new state of Scotland would have the political and economic power to insist upon membership; and Spanish objections based upon worries about the knock-on effect for Basque independence would probably be overridden by the more powerful European nations.)

Our new constitution also provides the British people with a new head of state, a federal president, this office being held by the head of state of the country holding the presidency of the Council of Ministers. This European president will have his or her own apparatus to organise the European Council; the president will chair the meetings of the Council and act as the new union's chief political spokesperson and chief diplomat. He or she will also preside at the ceremonial occasions of the new Europe. This new presidency will revolve among the twelve heads of government: British nationalists will see their own prime minister as president for six months every six years, but will also have to tolerate a German chancellor or Spanish prime minister becoming their president.

Another crucial aspect of the new union treaty – one which reinforces its character as a new constitution for the British – is that it sets out, US-style, how disputes and problems will be resolved by a Supreme Court. Our new Supreme Court – the European Court of Justice – will increasingly find itself having to adjudicate, not only between institutions of the union (Council, Commission and Parliament), but also between one national government and another, and between national governments and the union. It will do so, again US-style, on the basis of 'constitutionality' and in an environment in which European law takes precedence over British domestic law. It will also (under Article 171 of the treaty of union) be able to impose fines upon national governments.

In sum, the new union will, certainly legally, and over time politically too, become the ultimate constituted authority for the peoples of Europe. What is more, it will be overtly republican in character. The monarchs of Europe (the kings and queens of Britain, Spain, Belgium, Holland and Denmark) have no role at all in the new union; they have been dumped, written out of the union's structures by the large republics of Germany, Italy and France.

In this European republic of the twenty-first century, the norms of political dialogue will change dramatically. 'British politics', to the extent that it will continue as an organised and independent source of dispute, will of course continue to exhibit the old divisions between 'left', 'centre' and 'right'. Yet their conflicts will produce much less heat, and be conducted at a much lower level of intensity, as it becomes apparent that these alternative 'visions' can only properly be pursued within a broader European context. Similarly, the great technical economic dispute between Keynesians and monetarists, which has dominated British politics since the early 1970s, will continue, but will make sense only on a pan-European level. Economists, like businesses and other pressure groups, will be taking their case, and their ideas, to the European Central Bank (and the European Council's economic and finance ministers) in continental Europe.

Of course, party political organisation will still be needed in the nation-states, as it will be on a national basis that the governments sending ministers to the union in Brussels will be formed. Yet over time it is conceivable that, so intense will be the interest in the political flavour of the Council of Ministers or the Euro-Parliament, parties based, say, in Germany (through bodies like the Friedrich Ebert Stiftung or the Konrad Adenauer Stiftung) will help fund and organise campaigns in the south-east of England or the northern provinces of Italy. Thus the British will find their 'national debate' (and television coverage) increasingly 'invaded' by Euro-politicians – from German chancellors and French presidents to a host of lesser political functionaries – many of whom are likely to address the domestic audience in more comprehensible English than many of the homegrown politicos!

It seems likely that the great clashes of principle and ideas within British politics will no longer be about purely British issues, but instead will tend to centre on the European issue itself: between those who accept and those who resist this Europeanisation of British political life. Lord Cobbold, writing to *The Times* in 1992, suggested that in Britain 'the political divide of the future is between Europeans and nationalists', and argued, somewhat fancifully, though not incredibly, that a solution to the British imbroglio over Europe would be for the prime minister (any prime minister) completely to reconstruct British politics by making Europe a confidence issue, following which 'those voting for and against would then reconstruct themselves as new political parties. The winning side would elect a leader and form a government.'[2]

Of course, the new European union will be a dynamic and flexible polity. Nothing, except the fact of its existence, is set in stone. The American republic's character and pace of development depended not on some metaphysical centralised force, but rather on how the various institutions (president, Congress, courts and states) worked out their problems and their relations with one another. So, too, the decision about whether the union develops into a highly centralised, a looser 'federal', or an even looser 'confederal' system will evolve over time. The outcome will depend upon the interplay of political and economic forces over a host of issues, including harmonisation policies (for taxes and budgets); whether or not the union ultimately introduces its own taxes rather than continuing to precept on the national governments; and how the principles of 'subsidiarity' and 'mutual recognition' are interpreted. The British – their government, parties and interest groups – will have as serious a say as anyone else of comparable size and wealth, with much depending upon how they deploy the traditional political skills of alliance-making and coalition-building.

There is no reason why a fairly loose, federal structure should not emerge. ('Federal' is used here in the normal sense – that is, as used by Europeans, by British Liberals and by Americans – to denote a single central political authority co-existing with, and checked by, entrenched and powerful regions or states. Both the German Federal Republic and the United States are examples, whereas Britain and France, being over-centralised, with no 'built-in' powers for the regions, are not.) Alternatively, however, it is entirely possible that some of the worst fears of the Euro-sceptics will be realised, and a strongly centralised state will emerge out of the Maastricht process. Again, this will depend in part on the attitude taken by the Court of Justice. Like the US Supreme Court, it will inevitably be faced with a continuous flow of cases which will help it to define 'competencies' – where, for instance, an unrestricted national freedom to legislate lies and where it doesn't. Already it has been argued, by Gabriel M. Wilner, one of America's leading experts on European law, that:

> it is clear that the areas of community competence in economic and social matters are increasing at the expense of national power. The only powerful legal limitation to such expansion is likely to be the principle of subsidiarity, announced in the Maastricht agreement ... The two community courts [Court of Justice and Court of First Instance] will have an essential role in the application of subsidiarity to community acts.[3]

As with the new Americans in 1787, the new Europeans of the early 1990s cannot with any certainty foretell how their own new Supreme Court will settle down. What can be predicted, should the European union develop and cohere in a similar manner to that of the American republic, is that the Court of Justice will assume a much more prominent role than the founders ever envisaged. For instance, the decisive role of the Supreme Court as an agent of 'judicial review' – an arbiter of the powers of the executive and legislative branches – did not appear in the original constitution, but emerged through decisions of the Supreme Court itself (particularly in 'Marbury versus Madison' in 1803). And these decisions of the US Supreme Court, about subjects as varied as inter-state commerce and educational segregation, have changed the political and economic life of the United States more dramatically than any single act of Congress or president.

Yet no matter how centralised the European dynamic becomes, it will be as nothing compared to the London-based, centralised, and tightly controlled Leviathan that is Her Majesty's royal-state. For the European template, unlike the settlement of 1688 or the 1707 Act of Union, constitutionally limits the 'centre' (in Brussels) by *entrenching* the powers of other layers of government, particularly those of the nation-states. In a manner foreign to that dear old codger the UK (which could, within the time-span of a generation, both set up and abolish the Greater London Council), the new European executive must – by the force of a constitution and treaty – live, work and compromise with its 'regional' governments in the nation-states. And since all constitutions need improving, updating and amending (indeed, some of the more important changes in the life of republics like the US Bill of Rights, as well as some of the more bizarre, like the 1920 'prohibition' of alcohol, are the product of the amendment process), provision for this process has also been outlined in the treaty. As amendments to a constitution possess the full force of constitutional law – taking precedence over ordinary laws – many republics insist upon making the amendment process as difficult as possible by requiring referenda or two-thirds votes in the legislature, and so forth. (By contrast, Britain's royal-state has no formal amendment procedure: the unwritten constitution can be changed by a single Act of Parliament, passed by a majority of one.) The Maastricht treaty ensures that the new European republic will need to achieve unanimity among its member states before an amendment can go through.

'Amending' the Maastricht treaty may indeed be the mechanism chosen by the new Europeans as they seek to give the new Euro-constitution both flesh and life. The most urgent area in need of improvement is the continuing European 'democratic deficit'. Maastricht gave the European Parliament powers of 'co-decision' over law-making in the union – a significant advance – but the new Europe still appears very executive-driven. Not until the European Parliament has the kind of powers available to the US Congress – in law-making, in financial appropriations, in investigatory procedures – will it have arrived as a main player. The German government, during the Maastricht debates, took the lead in attempting to give the Euro Parliament more powers (and Her Majesty's government in the royal-state led the resistance); nothing less than the future of the democratic culture of the union depends upon whether the authorities in Bonn can command a coalition which will further extend the Euro Parliament's powers.

'Democracy' is not just about voting and legislatures. It is equally about entrenching the rights of the individual against the state. The founders of the new union, like the founders in Philadelphia some two centuries earlier, need to round out their constitution-making by creating a regime of rights that is broader and deeper than the limited rights (of movement, residence, voting and diplomatic protection) drawn up at Maastricht. The best way to do this is fully to incorporate the European Convention on Human Rights into the governing constitution of the European union, although this hugely important liberal advance has so far been dodged by this generation of Euro-politicians.

The problem facing British politicians in Europe is that the condition of the 'democratic deficit' in their own UK royal-state effectively disables them from making a serious democratic critique of the European union. Yet both Tory right and Labour

166

left still tend to unite in a culture of anti-union rebuke –
while at the same time resisting proposals for enhancing the
democracy of Europe (particularly the Parliament) because of
their 'federal' or 'super-state' implications.

Will Britain make it?

Will Britain's politicians be able to take part in the construction
of the new European political entity? Or will the habits and
attitudes instilled by the culture of the royal-state leave them
– sour, pompous and stand-offish – on the margins?

One area where British political input has been unusually
positive is in the attempt, led by John Major at the 1992
Edinburgh summit, to place the issue of 'openness' (of central
institutions like the Commission and Council) on the immediate
European political agenda. Of course, here again, Britain does
not practise what it preaches (as we have seen, royal-state
politicians inhabit one of the most secretive political regimes
in the West, let alone Europe), yet these 'glasnost' proposals
are a sign that some within the British political class can on
occasion think constructively about the new political system
enfolding them.

The biggest test of Britain's commitment to the new European
union will come, however, not in the country's involvement in
Brussels, but rather in its ability to Europeanise the residual
structures of the old royal-state – that is, to make Britain's
domestic constitutional arrangements fit in with the new union.
Britain's tax-payers cannot be asked to fund several levels of
government for ever, especially given that some of them are
becoming increasingly or wholly redundant. Even in the absence
of any serious reform of the UK royal-state, 'Whiteminster' will
be under pressure to make some consequential changes in order
to align itself with the new union. Reducing the size of the House
of Commons and the House of Lords, reallocating the Whitehall
civil service to European functions, and formally linking the
domestic courts to the European system (by establishing a similar
relationship to that between federal and state courts in the USA)

are all early candidates for action. Earliest of all, and much to the dismay of the royal-state's Treasury and the Chancellor of the Exchequer, a British independent central bank will need to be approved by Parliament by the time the putative European system of central banks is set up.[4]

Whether Britain operates at 'the very heart of Europe' or is marginalised (technically a full member of the union, but in reality excluded from the inner core of members, and thus subject to policy though not participating in its formulation) will depend upon the prosaic workings of the British economy. It will be economic criteria that determine whether, in the assessment meetings scheduled for 1996, Britain is nominated by the European Council as one of the minimum of seven member-states needed to 'fulfil the necessary conditions for the adoption of a single currency', or whether it is subjected to a humiliating 'derogation'.[5] This will depend on the politics of the Council at the time and the extent to which Britain has met the 'convergence indicators'. But even before stage 2 of monetary union (beginning in January 1994, and a stage for which Britain has secured no 'opt out'), Britain will have been required to 'adopt . . . multi-annual programmes intended to ensure the lasting convergence necessary for the achievement of economic and monetary union, in particular with regard to price stability and sound public finances'.[6] In this stage Britain 'shall endeavour to avoid excessive government deficits' and start the process leading to the independence of its central bank, within a regime in which a European Central Bank (the European Monetary Institute) is born.

Thus by D-Day – some time before 1 July 1998, the last possible date for the beginning of stage 3 of Economic and Monetary Union – Britain will already have been existing under an economic and monetary regime determined by the need to 'converge'. According to one survey based upon statistics supplied by the European Commission, Britain 'qualified' under three of the 'convergence indicators' (long-term interest rates, the budget deficit and the national debt), and failed on two (the rate of inflation and the exchange-rate provisions).[7]

In one sense, then, the political will to meet economic

'convergence criteria' is more immediately important than that needed to 'converge' constitutionally. An early test of this 'will' will come over the question of the pound sterling's re-entry into the ERM, which will need to take place at least two years ahead of the 'great examination' of 1996.[8]

A more open society

There is a sense in which Britain's integration into the European union will result in more radical change at home than all the progressive campaigning of a hundred years. Increasingly, even domestic British opinion is coming to understand that the royal-state's 'pretension to rule is increasingly undermined by external forces, particularly the European Community', and that 'this is probably the largest single reason for change in Britain, working not only through the direct influence of the Community on British law and commerce, but also by exposing British society more directly to alternative ideas and ways of doing things'.[9]

Of course, the union's most momentous service will be to remove the royal-state constitution from the backs of the British people. The coming immersion in Europe will alter the way we think about and relate to one another, our perceived positions in society, our attitudes towards status and influence – in other words, the vitals of Britain's stubborn class sensibilities. For instance, Britain's highly centralised and structured social system can only be weakened by a revival of provincial and local sentiment, something Europe can help to do, by ensuring that the London-based 'institutions of England' lose their authority and legitimacy, and that the regions and nations of the old royal-state are able to deal directly with Brussels. In the new US-style, continent-wide, pluralist, 'log-rolling' network of centre–regional relationships, the old London-based centres of power over the British are likely to be drowned out, marginalised in their influence on the future course of Britain's life.

Over time, the wider union will help to erode many of the domestic British restrictive practices that limit consumer choice.

169

An early example presents itself in the public health area. EC laws and directives are insisting that surgeons from other EC countries should be able to compete with British surgeons within the NHS. Such competition is seen as a dagger at the heart of the cosy world of BMA medical privilege, and the British medical establishment is attempting a rearguard action by declaring that continental surgeons will bring in their wake 'lower standards'. This early breeze in what will become a lasting burst of competitive fresh air will be duplicated throughout a thousand 'nooks and crannies' of the cosseted world of British restrictive practices. And of course, in return for accepting greater competition domestically, Britain's professionals (providing they achieve certain language skills) will be able to compete on the continent in a market of over 300 million: potentially, at least, a career and life move well worth making, and one which will contribute to a further loosening of the loyalties that tie a population to its monarchy.

This widening of horizons – both geographically and intellectually – is the real boon which Europe gives to those British subjects who will take seriously their role as newly emerging citizens of the union. Earlier this century, the American historian Frederick Jackson Turner argued that 'the rise of the new West was the most significant fact in American history'.[10] The contemporary Britons will also benefit from a new 'frontier'. They may do so by taking advantage of many of the practical opportunities – for jobs and careers – which a huge, economically advanced internal market provides. But just as important will be the *idea* of being part of a continental civilisation stretching from Ireland to Greece and from Scandinavia to Gibraltar. This new 'continental imagination' – with its liberating sense of space and possibility – might, never mind that most Britons will stay at home, help towards a change in the constrictedness and sense of limitation within the domestic social climate.

The paternalism of the royal-state thrived on the fact that its subjects were confined within the boundaries of the island home. Now, mass travel, transferability of professional qualifications, ever closer (though competitive) commercial and financial relations – even intra-national marriages – all these things, and more, will give the new generation of Britons a liberating sense of space, of frontier, and of opportunity. This new culture will have its effect on the domestic circumstances of Britain, putting further pressure for change upon the culture of the royal-state.

10 · A British Republic

In a sense, the issue of a new written constitution for the British becomes redundant. After all, it would, outside of a British decision to withdraw from the union, need to comply with the rules of the federal union, and thus would, in essence, simply become a localised and domesticated version of the Maastricht framework. For instance, the proposal for a new British written constitution from the Liberal Party includes, as we have seen, the creation of a Supreme Court on the American model, which would 'strike down legislation which it deems unconstitutional, curb the power of the executive, resolve disputes between the [British] Federal Parliament, national parliaments and regional assemblies over their respective powers, and protect the rights of citizens guaranteed by the Bill of Rights'.[1] Yet such a British domestic Supreme Court would essentially be subordinate to the European Court, and could only act rather like an American state Supreme Court: in declaring legislation and executive actions unconstitutional, it would also have to apply superior federal (European) law, as well as any domestic British law.

Even so, the arguments for an independent British constitutional revolution, in which the British themselves replace the royal-state and create their own domestic republican constitution, are overwhelming. For a start, Britain will need a new written constitution as an insurance policy against just the eventuality I mention above – should, that is, some major political cataclysm overcome the European union, leading to its member states separating off. There is also something rather undignified about Britain having to resort to creating a modern constitution by an Act of treaty and ratification. 'Constitution-making by treaty' is, obviously, better than nothing; but a domestic written constitution would give the new union's constitution even greater legitimacy. And why not reinforce at every level – particularly the British level – the new constitutional settlement?

The making of a new British constitution which could replace the royal-state and its monarchy overnight would be fairly straightforward. There are two possible routes. First, a new constitution could be enacted by using the existing system of parliamentary sovereignty and passing a Bill – like Tony Benn's Commonwealth of Britain Bill, which incorporates a new written constitution – through the House of Commons, thus challenging the Lords and monarch to veto it. Like the Lords over eighty years ago, the two hereditary branches would find this difficult to refuse. The Liberal Democrats have suggested that, should this route be taken, then the whole procedure should be conducted over two Parliaments. The first Parliament would pass a 'Constituent Assembly Act' to provide for 'the House of Commons elected at the subsequent election to sit as a Constituent Assembly, charged with drawing up a written constitution for the UK, incorporating the reforms set out in this paper; the constitution to be amendable only by two-thirds majorities of both [the new] Houses of Parliament'.[2]

The alternative route is to 'ratify' a new written constitution by referendum. A reform-minded House of Commons could draw up the new constitution and then submit it to the electors; upon receiving a majority (or two-thirds), it would become the governing constitution of Britain.

By enacting a new written constitution, all the institutions of the erstwhile royal-state would come under law, and exist at the pleasure of the constitution. For Britain formally to become a republic, all that would be needed would be to ensure that in the new written constitution the clause referring to the head of state did not base the office on the hereditary principle. It is no more difficult than this to dissolve the Crown and bring to an end a thousand years of royal-state history!

Of course, Britain could abolish the monarchy and become a republic *without* enacting a written constitution by an Act of Parliament replacing the monarch by a president (and including consequential clauses about oaths, the armed forces, and the residual status and financing of the royal family).

But whether Britain becomes a republic by virtue of a new written constitution, or simply by an Act of Parliament, any new settlement will affect some of the most historically revered institutions of British constitutional life. Any institution or ritual based upon hereditary symbolism will go: after the monarchy itself, that will include the hereditary element in the House of Lords, the Privy Council, and the existing relationship between the monarch and the Church and the armed services. The Church of England could dispense with the post of 'Supreme Governor', and would probably vest the minimal powers the monarchy once possessed in the Archbishop of Canterbury. The armed forces would no longer owe loyalty to the sovereign, but rather, through a new oath, to the state, or the constitution; and the military leadership would report solely up the chain of command – to the minister of defence and thence to the prime minister or president (depending upon whether the president was both chief executive and head of state). New hereditary titles would cease to be awarded, and existing hereditary titles would no longer possess constitutional sanction. Should hereditary peers wish to continue to describe themselves by their erstwhile hereditary title, then they would be free to do so – but any citizen could call themselves what they like ('Count Basie', should they wish). Whatever happened to the upper House, feudal designations would no longer be officially recognised – but, again, people would remain free to call themselves whatever they wish.

A republican form of government is not a confiscatory regime. All it would demand would be for every citizen to be treated equally under the law, so that although there would be no monarch, no royal family, no officially sanctioned hereditary titles nor hereditary members of the legislature, the property, wealth and income of these erstwhile peers would be unaffected – they would be treated in exactly the same manner as anyone else. And as for the ex-monarch and ex-royal family, they too would simply become citizens, like everyone else. As these ex-royals have a special relationship to the state and the Exchequer, some kind of financial settlement would be needed. Presumably, although the ex-royal family would no longer reside and function at the state palaces, they would continue to live in their privately owned palaces. There would need to be a settlement of all the assets – like the royal jewellery collection and the royal paintings – whose ownership is ambiguous. Also, some final decision would need to be taken about the validity of the title to the Duchies of Cornwall and Lancaster (perhaps by a court case) before their final ownership was settled. Whatever final settlement was reached, the ex-royals would remain among the richest people in the new republic – and, of course, like anyone else, they could continue to call themselves by their previous titles. Elizabeth Windsor could still, should she wish, call herself 'the Queen', and Charles Windsor 'the King' (but so too could anyone else).

Should a republic be established by an Act of Parliament, rather than by a new written constitution, all the other institutions of the country would function in exactly the same manner as before, with only symbolic changes affecting their operations. It would no longer be 'Her Majesty's courts' (instead, simply 'courts'), 'Her Majesty's Government' (instead, simply the British government), 'Her Majesty's Loyal Opposition' (simply 'the Opposition'). The post office would be free to issue stamps without the monarch's head on them, and similarly with the minting of coins and notes. 'Her Majesty's Inspectors of Schools' and 'Her Majesty's Inspectors of Taxes' would lose the royal appellation. 'Royal Charters' (issued for universities) would simply become 'parliamentary charters'. Awards would continue to be made to those deemed to merit them although, hopefully, feudal and imperial terminology would be dropped. The president would receive diplomats, take the salute at national ceremonials, and would open Parliament.

The royal prerogative powers – the powers now vested in

the monarch and the executive to make treaties, declare war, and award honours and so forth – would, in the minimalist republican option, probably be distributed between the government and Parliament and, of course, the institutions of the European union. In a full-scale new republican written constitution, they would probably be vested in the legislature.

'Blood ordinary'

For the next few years, the main difficulty with securing a republican form of government, should there be a majority of the public in favour of it, will be the seemingly intractable, 'immovable object' of the Queen herself, by comparison with which dissolving those other pillars of the royal-state – the House of Lords and the establishment of the Church – would be easy! Only when the Queen goes will an opportunity arise – especially given the unlikelihood of a national consensus in favour of a new 'reign': that of Charles III. The heir to the throne does not command widespread public support – certainly nowhere near that secured by his mother at the time of her coronation. This is not surprising. Even Walter Bagehot can give him little hope:

> The case is worse when he [a Prince] comes to [the monarchy] old or middle aged. He is then unfit to work. He will then have spent the whole of youth and the first part of manhood in idleness, and it is unnatural to expect him to labour . . . The only fit material for a constitutional king is a prince who begins early to reign . . . Such kings are among God's greatest gifts, but they are also among his rarest.[3]

Of course, Charles may for purely personal reasons resign ahead of his coronation, or, should he get that far, abdicate soon after it. Any attempt to 'skip a generation' by sliding the succession to William would seem (particularly if engineered ahead of Charles's death) far too contrived. But whatever happens, there is no doubt that the royal family and the

176

monarchy will, at the time of the next accession, be highly controversial.

Those in Parliament who, even with public opinion running swiftly in favour of radical change, will not wish to brook Elizabeth Windsor, have a way out. They can argue that Parliament should take the opportunity of the next few years to think through (and agree) the outlines of a written constitution which would be implemented only when the reign of Elizabeth II comes to an end. Of course, this does not mean that Elizabeth Windsor would lend her name to any such parliamentary discussion. But if Britain's political class, because of this, refuse to place the question on the agenda, the effect would be simply to bottle up public indignation, leading to a much higher wave of public sentiment some years later. There will come a time when a senior political figure, or a party faction, or a party itself, takes up the issue. All that will be needed is for one of the three parties to present a set of anti-monarchist policy proposals (even if they are not overtly republican); this posture will lead either to other parties supporting the proposals, in which case a republican future is ratcheted up a notch or two, or to the parties dividing on the issue – a development which will make the monarchy a partisan player in the politics of the nation.

Any decision to replace the monarchy by a presidency would need also to resolve the question of the character of the new office. Among the constitutional reform groups, the only organisation which has studied the issue, with a view to suggesting the most appropriate form for Britain, is the republican society, Republic. It argues that the country needs to make a straight choice between an executive presidency (as in the USA and France) or a non-executive presidency (as in Germany and Ireland). Should Britain opt for an executive presidency, then the new office (which would need to be elected) would, as in the USA, become a major political player, part of a system of separated powers, and checked within a written constitution by a powerful legislature and constitutional court.

Republic itself suggests that a non-executive presidency would be best, because the present British system could more easily adapt to it than to the overtly political institution operating in the United States. The role proposed for this non-executive presidency would be similar to that carried through by the Queen (representing the country, accrediting diplomats and so forth), though with some crucial differences – such as the removal of the prerogative powers and the abandonment of the personalised oath. (Republic argues that pledges of allegiance made by members of the armed forces, MPs, judges, and any other public officials required to make such a pledge should be made instead to 'the constitution'.[4]) This non-executive presidency could be elected (as in Ireland) or nominated (probably by the legislature, as in Germany), but for a largely ceremonial post a direct national election would not really be necessary. In this model, of course, the Speaker of the House of Commons could become president, or, alternatively, the person elected to the chair of the upper House could assume the role.

Some criticism of the notion of a British presidency has rested upon the idea that it would become 'politicised', that is, manned by partisan political officeholders. Yet should the presidency be executive in nature, simple democratic practice would demand a 'politicised' presidency (that is, an 'elected' presidency). Should the presidency be non-executive, then there would be no need for it to be 'politicised': indeed, political people could compete with artists, scientists, academics, business people or trade unionists for the honour. Contrary to the belief that in a nation of 55 million there is no single person available who could perform the role as well as Elizabeth Windsor, the country can expect to have a wide choice. (Should the legislature make the choice, it would perhaps tend to be a person drawn from the 'political' side of public life.)

The new president of Britain would not (as is the Queen) be president for life. His or her tenure would be for a short period only, and arguably for one term only, and this crucial change would be symbolic. The new president would represent the people, not the separated, mystical entity of 'the Crown', and would be pledged to 'uphold the constitution', not a dynastic

House; after a period in office, he or she would simply return to ordinary life.

The republican virtues

Britain's two most prominent nineteenth-century republicans, Joseph Chamberlain and Sir Charles Dilke, both saw the formal creation of a republic in Britain as less important than the spread of republican virtues. And they were surprisingly similar in their depiction of these virtues. Dilke, speaking in Leeds in November 1872, on the very night of the public announcement of the Prince of Wales's illness, which would help scupper the burst of republicanism that he led, argued that:

> [the] promotion by merit alone and . . . the non-recognition of any claims founded upon birth – is commonly accepted as republican. I care not whether you call it republican or whether you do not, but I say that it is the only principle upon which, if we are to keep our place among the nations, we can for the future act.[5]

For his part, Chamberlain, speaking three weeks later, was more equivocal than Dilke on the institutional question of abolishing the monarchy, but just as firm and clear on the central principle of republicanism:

> The idea, to my mind, that underlies Republicanism is this: that in all cases merit should have a fair chance, that it should not be handicapped in the race by accident of birth or privilege; that all men should have equal rights before the law, equal chances of serving their country.[6]

These liberal notions – of the imperatives of merit and the need for political, though not necessarily economic, equality – have fuelled the radical imagination in the modern era. This is why the hereditary principle – that wealth, income, status and position can be unearned, based solely upon 'the accident of

179

birth' – is treated with distaste, and political rights based upon heredity are so fiercely opposed by republicans.

A republic would insist upon 'equality before the law'. Everyone over the designated age (including the Queen, members of the royal family and peers) would have the vote, and everyone (including the Queen and members of the royal family) would be subject to the laws. Everyone, irrespective of their social background (or 'rank') would be able to aspire to all the various awards and honours. There would be no special political privileges, no separate classes of citizens.

A philosophy which advocates a generalised 'anti-heredity' position naturally runs into problems. Does republicanism oppose leaving assets and money to family? Should children not gain an educational advantage (say, by going to private schools) because they happen to be born into a particular family? Is it a republican position that the natural inequalities of life based upon the random fact of birth should be equalised as much as possible? Yet these questions are, essentially, the stuff of traditional political debate, between right and left; they are *not* the gravamen of the republican case. It is probably the case that republicans would have a 'predilection' towards earned rather than unearned resources, but this is not the essence of the matter, because for republicans the issue is the link between *heredity* and *government*. It is essentially a political, not an economic, belief: no matter what might occur in the private, or economic, sphere, 'official', 'public', 'constitutional' life should be free from inequalities based upon lineage. Above all, the political and constitutional world should reflect the basic political equality of humankind. In politics at least – as they vote, as they participate, as they govern, above all simply by virtue of being a citizen – all humans have equal worth, 'all men are created equal'.

The vision of one of the greatest of all republicans (in both party and philosophic senses of the term), Abraham Lincoln, provides perhaps the nearest definition of the term that we can come to. A reading of his Gettysburg Address would give the drift in poetic form, but what it all amounts to is a belief in the idea of citizenship, of free, independent men and women, possessed of equal political rights and freedoms, determining their own government. In other words: the basic postulates behind the modern liberal conception of democracy.

Fundamental to any republican system is the idea that the people own their own state. The idea of government by 'the people' first took hold in the ancient Greek republics, and Pericles argued, in the fifth century BC, that 'our constitution is called a democracy because power is in the hands not of a minority but of the whole people'. Of course, in the modern era the Americans started it all. In the preamble to their constitution, we read: 'We *the People* of the United States . . . do ordain and establish this Constitution for the United States of America.' The French soon followed suit, and today, in the Fifth Republic, 'National Sovereignty belongs to *the people* who shall exercise it through their representatives and by way of referendum.'[7] In the modern German constitution, 'all state authority emanates from *the people*'.[8] And in the republican ideal, 'We, the people . . . ordain and establish' that other crucial republican requirement: a written constitution, establishing a clear and understandable line of democratic authority.

Unfortunately, unlike its American constitutional counterpart, the Maastricht treaty is no easy read. It has few ringing phrases, it is convoluted and often very technical. Yet it exists. And because it is written, and can therefore be discovered, it marks a sharp departure from the obscurantism of the British royal-state.

The core virtue of the republican system of government is citizenship, and the basic rights attaching to citizenship. Until the British introduce their own domestic republic, we will need to rely upon the citizenship established for Britons by the new union treaty: 'Citizenship of the Union is hereby established. Every person holding the nationality of a member state shall be a citizen of the union . . . Citizens of the union shall enjoy the rights conferred by this treaty . . .'[9] Thus, for the very first time, Queen Elizabeth and the royal family become 'citizens of the union', on an equal basis with every other British national.

Even before the new union gave a huge boost to the role of the European Court, the European regime of rights was forcing its way into British life. In a landmark case, Mrs Jackie

Drake – who had been refused an invalid care allowance for looking after her elderly mother, even though a man in the same situation would have received one – took her case to the court on the grounds of sex discrimination. She won; and the British government was forced to comply. Another sex discrimination case involved one Mr Barber, who was made redundant at 52 but discovered that he could not draw his pension until he was 62; a woman in exactly his position would have been entitled to a pension at the point of redundancy, and he won his case, though, sadly, posthumously. In yet another case Helen Marshall (in much the same manner as would an American citizen who feels discriminated against) challenged the legality of her dismissal from her job when she was 62 (because of a compulsory retirement rule) on the grounds that men could work until 65. Yet again, the court supported the British subject against the British state, and the UK government was forced to change its rules.[10]

Such cases, involving many other rights beyond those against sex discrimination, can be expected to multiply. However, it is not the weight of the case load that is important: what will make the difference is a few historic cases, which will not only force national governments to change their rules, but will lead them to act pre-emptively over a whole range of law. According to Gabriel Wilner, the European Court of Justice may be poised to take a lead in forging a new constitutional culture. Already, through an 'expansive reading of the powers of the institutions of the European Communities [the European Court of Justice] has acted very much like John Marshall's Supreme Court [in the United States] in the early nineteenth century.'[11]

However, the rights conferred by the union treaty on union citizens are still fairly limited. Every citizen will have the right to move and reside freely within the union, and possess rights of candidature, voting and diplomatic protection. Beyond this there is, as yet, no formal, entrenched Bill of Rights for citizens. But buried in the small print of the treaty is a clause which is potentially revolutionary. For the union's founders have virtually incorporated the European Convention for the Protection of Human Rights into the body of European co-operation on civil and criminal law, and have certainly opened the way for a future European Court (in its power to 'interpret the treaty') to develop future law.[12] Thus, whether the European Convention on Human Rights is ultimately fully incorporated in the new union or not, the fact of its existence puts the British establishment firmly on the spot. Britons will still have to go through the humiliating exercise of going abroad to achieve the rights of citizenship; and this can only mean that, over time, questions will start being asked about why such rights are not available at home. As the feel of citizenship emerges among the British, the question may become more and more insistent, while the answer from the British establishment is bound to remain obscure. But in any event, the regime of rights, which through the European Convention and the new union is beginning to make itself felt, represents a kind of vindication for Britain's great wayward liberal son, Tom Paine. His 'Rights of Man' is coming home at last.

There is now a real possibility that a culture of openness may be created through the European union, even though 'rights to information' are unlikely to be high on the agenda of the European Court. Most European politicians seem willing to pay obeisance to the idea of an open society, and already the Committee of Ministers of the Council of Europe have recommended that member states improve their access record:

Everyone within the jurisdiction of a member state shall have a right to obtain, on request, information held by the public authorities other than legislative bodies and judicial authorities.

Effective and appropriate means shall be provided to ensure access to information.

Access to information shall not be refused on the grounds that the requesting person has not a specific interest in the matter.

A public authority refusing access to information shall give the reasons on which the refusal is based, according to law and practice.

183

Any refusal of information shall be subject to review on request.[13]

In a republican system, the rights of citizens are not only protected by formal, codified, entrenched constitutional provisions, but also by the 'the separation of powers'. The idea here is that 'overlapping institutions', like 'overlapping directorships', can be bad for the citizen's health. Thus, ideally, the executive, legislature and judiciary should be separate, creating a pluralistic culture of governance which both limits the power of any one institution, and provides the individual with some manoeuvrability.

Of course, many republics possess parliamentary systems, and therefore the executive branch is *not* separated from the legislature. In these cases (Germany being a prime example) the separation of institutions is ensured, not only by the federal system itself (in which powers are divided up between Bonn and the *Länder*), but also by a written constitution in which a Federal Constitutional Court can limit the powers of any institution of the state.

Used to living in an environment with highly concentrated power and centralised authority, the British political class may find it difficult, initially at least, to adjust to living in a less ordered and hierarchical political society, with innumerable 'checks and balances'. At first it will seem confusing, often even chaotic. Yet Americans have lived with such a system for over two hundred years, and in the process have developed a highly stable democratic system. In any event, the British will be entering a more plural and separated system as they take part in the new European union, and as old institutions, like the monarchy, the Lords and Commons, compete with new Euro-institutions, not only for the citizen's support, but also for their tax pounds, or ecus. And a competitive separation of powers will also exist at 'federal' level between the Commission, the Council, the Parliament and the Court. Never will there have been so many competing power centres; 'confusing' and 'chaotic', certainly, but, for the individual, a great leap forward in limiting government by 'dividing and ruling' it.

England without the monarch

By the early 1990s – with republicanism emerging at home and the new union establishing itself in Europe – the lifespan of the monarchy (and its associated royal-state) was beginning to look somewhat limited. It was even suggested that what the country was witnessing was the reign of 'Elizabeth the Last,'[14] a prospect that no longer seemed so terrifying to large numbers of British people. Certainly many Scots were not worried, and neither were large numbers of Welsh (the Celtic parts of Britain had always seen the monarchy as essentially English and remote). But even in England, the supposed homeland of British monarchy, it was only a significant minority (albeit many of them among the most influential and established groups in the country) who still perceived republicanism as a threat. The menace, unlike socialism, was not financial; it involved no schemes for redistribution of wealth or income, no reallocation of resources. Rather, the threat to what Sampson called 'the whole security of the nation' was to identity, to meaning, to a notion of 'Englishness' itself.

Of course, to any well-balanced Englishman or woman the idea that his or her identity would be affected by the loss of monarchy would not be out of place in the theatre of the absurd. Bernard Crick suggested that he, for one, could not believe 'that Englishness [was] nothing but an illusory worship of the Crown as an imperial symbol'; he also believed 'the English would remain English, for better or worse, with or without the Crown'.[15] England will remain England. Life will go on. Cottages and pubs and churches, council houses and high-rise blocks and bingo halls, the Tower of London, the Palace of Westminster, Buckingham Palace, Anfield and Highbury, Lords (the cricket ground, that is), the BBC, the ITV, even the tabloids – all these and more will still be there when there is no monarch on the throne. Yet even if England will still be there, will the sense of Englishness? Is there, in truth, any such thing as Englishness? Is there an English identity which binds together all those who live in England and excludes all those who don't? Is there, in other words, anything to lose, except an illusion?

There is, of course, an easily identifiable cultural type which has pretensions to represent Englishness. This is what might be called the stage-Englishman and stage-Englishwoman, the 'county and tweeds' and 'city and bowler' type. This is the stereotype which the royal family have both created and attempted, somewhat self-consciously, to portray; yet very few real English people resemble this type at all, and such stage-Englishness is utterly unrepresentative of anything outside its tiny circle. Even so, many English people certainly believe that such an identity exists, and that it is somehow threatened by the 'non-Englishness' of foreigners, and in an organised manner by the European union. Of all the countries polled in a 1992 survey, it was the British who displayed less 'European feeling' than any other member country of the union. Whereas 60 per cent of Germans and 52 per cent of French feel European 'often' or 'sometimes', only 28 per cent of Britons do. The British were also last in 'feeling a citizen of Europe'.[16]

Of course, these figures may not reflect any widespread sensibility of Englishness, but rather a more universal human fear about the loss of established and familiar ways of life. And what may make the British stand out – among other Europeans – in their rejection of change is that these normal fears are exaggerated, worked on and legitimised by powerful elements in Britain's polity. For centuries high Tory ideology has told a captive people that the familiar is good for you and that, beyond a point, change should be resisted. Aided, often subconsciously, by its revered institutions, particularly the monarchy, it has bred among a wider public a corpus of social conservatism, provincialism and backwardness, not just as a reactionary impulse but also as a cute way of life.

Ultimately, whether such a thing as Englishness actually exists rests crucially upon whether the inhabitants of England are anything more than a collection of individuals and families inhabiting the same state structure, or whether they are, in truth, a family. George Orwell was a prominent exponent of the theory of 'the nation as family', and he made it sound very cosy:

It is a family in which the young are generally thwarted and most of the power is in the hands of irresponsible uncles and bedridden aunts. Still it is a family. It has its private language and common memories, and at the approach of an enemy it closes its ranks. A family with the wrong members in control – that, perhaps, is as near as one can come in describing England in a phrase.[17]

A family needs a head, and in Orwell's English family that position is held by the monarch. Yet this analogy is misplaced. The English no longer, if they ever did, resemble the tight-knit, homogeneous, empathetic characteristics associated with the idealised family. Instead of a single English identity, the contemporary reality is more a composite of a large number of separate identities – Geordie, Scouse, Muslim, Brummie, West Indian, Cornish, East Anglian, Cockney – the list is endless. To ask whether in any real sense all these distinctive groups possess a commonality of identity which lumps them together, separates them from other peoples, and can properly be represented by a tribal headship like the House of Windsor, is to answer the question: of course they don't. To believe, for instance, that a bank official living in Reading has more in common with, say, his fellow compatriot the Duke of Westminster (or Prince Charles) than he has with his opposite number in France, Germany or America is bordering on the disturbed.

In fact the English – and more certainly still the British – have, by modern standards, a very weak sense of national identity. This may help explain why in the great European debate the British, unlike, say, the French or Luxemburgers, remain so insecure and defensive about nationhood. People with a coherent and confident sense of themselves tend not worry about the possibility of losing it.

Looking to the future, whatever national identity may yet remain will, in all probability, be further eroded by mass communications and the spread of information and travel, until the whole of the West (as well as the whole of Europe) resembles a single civilisation possessing an increasingly blurred cultural identity. The remaining aspect of culture that still separates the British from others within the Western world (particularly the Europeans of the union), and which naturally and genuinely reinforces the sense of national identity, is language. The English language is indeed a commonality for the peoples of Britain, shared by all (like the monarchy and the royal-state they live under). However, the English language is a universal phenomenon, spoken by foreigners often as proficiently and eloquently as many speakers of the 'mother tongue'. Translations are becoming more freely available, as is language teaching. And the English are lucky in one respect, for English will probably become the informal *lingua franca* of the new union, and the primary language of those who travel and move and do business in Europe.

Although national identity is now, to all intents and purposes, a thing of the past in Britain, a sense of nation, or national sentiment, or even patriotism will continue as a reality. For what endures beyond the death of the formal structures of the nation-state is the universal human regard and fondness for background, for locale, for the places of one's upbringing. As the rationalist Ernest Gellner has suggested, 'patriotism is a perennial part of human life . . . while nationalism is a very distinctive species of patriotism'.[18] Gellner also suggests that nationalism is essentially the product of modern times, and, being transitory, may now be on the way out.

If Gellner is only half-right, and the ideological and obsessive aspects of nationalism so prevalent during Britain's declining years are in the process of dissolution, then so too is the navel-contemplating obsession with 'Englishness', leaving us to settle down and understand that to be English is simply to live in this island, to share it, and the state which covers it, with others. In such an England, one 'at peace with itself', life without the monarchy would not be something to explain away, but rather would seem natural and right.

Elizabeth the last

Britain will soon come face to face with its republican future. It will not come suddenly, but it will surprise no one, and will probably follow on the heels of the establishment of an Australian republic. Republican sentiment is bound to grow in Australia in the years leading up to the new century, and no matter the government in power it now seems inconceivable that Australians will remain subjects to the monarchy for much longer. In one of the several drafts of the potential new Australian constitution, prepared by Professor George Winterton of the University of New South Wales for the Australian Republican Movement, the existing 1900 constitution is used, with a few simple amendments such as deleting 'the Queen' and 'the Governor-General' and inserting 'the President'. Australia's constitutional position will in its turn affect Canada and New Zealand.

The transition from monarchy to republic in Britain can, as we have seen, be secured without upheaval. On the other hand, it could become a traumatic experience. Much depends upon the attitude of the present Queen. Should she decide to ride out the present crisis by making no fundamental alteration to the role and style of the monarchy (and only reform piecemeal, as a response to public pressure), then republican sentiment will grow very quickly indeed, causing a polarisation of views in which the monarchy becomes a partisan issue. But even should a major reform of the monarchy be engineered, republican sentiment is unlikely to be appeased. It would have tasted blood; the monarchy would no longer seem invincible; and in the new, more democratic and egalitarian environment the fundamental critique of constitutional heredity would possess even greater force. What is more, for as long as Britain retains any kind of monarchy, the royal family will remain centre-stage, a constant target of criticism.

The most sensible way forward is for Britain's political leadership to resolve that, following the death or abdication of Elizabeth Windsor, she would have been Elizabeth the Last, and the country should become a republic. The Queen could play a part, in the final years of her reign, in helping to smooth the way for the constitutional transition, perhaps assisted by her son, whose views on the role of the monarchy in a modern society could be expressed as widely as he liked. Should the

Windsors be able to take such a lead and finally help put the British monarchy to rest, then nothing would become them like this last act of service.

Yet no matter how the Queen and the royal family decide to respond to monarchy's crisis, Britain's political class can use it as an opportunity. There is a sense in which, on the verge not only of a new millennium, but of a new role in Europe, the country is at a historic turning point. Britain as a republic could represent a fresh start, a chance to lay to rest our final symbolic link to a past which holds us back, not only from creating a democratic society open to all talents, but also from competing effectively in the world.

Abolishing the monarchy will not solve all the country's problems. What it will do, though, is remove what amounts to an institutionalised focus for all the backward social and cultural attitudes that have bedevilled Britain for a century or more. By removing the fount of backwardness, a modern, open and competitive society may at least have a chance to emerge.

References

Introduction

1 Gallup survey for the *Daily Telegraph*, 22 February 1993.
2 Piers Brendon, in the *New Statesman*, 11 December 1992, has reported: 'recently, a millionaire entrepreneur told me that his friend Margaret Thatcher agreed with him that Britain could never make progress until it abolished the monarchy'.
3 This 'option' was already being canvassed by liberal opinion as 1992 closed.
4 Article 1 of Sweden's 1974 constitution.

1 Whatever Happened to 'The Good Old Cause'?

1 Christopher Hill, *God's Englishman* (Weidenfeld & Nicolson, London, 1970), p. 13.
2 'Democratic republicans' is the term used by Christopher Hill to describe the Levellers; see Hill, *Milton and the English Revolution* (Penguin, London, 1979), p. 95.
3 Ibid., p. 189.
4 Milton, *The Ready and Easy Way to Establish a Free Commonwealth*, quoted ibid.
5 For a discussion of Locke's radicalism, see Richard Ashcroft,

'Simple Objections and Complex Reality: Theorising Political Radicalism in Seventeenth-century England', *Political Studies*, xi (1992), pp. 99–115.

6 J. H. Plumb, *The Growth of Political Stability in England, 1675–1725* (Penguin, London, 1967), p. 187.

7 Hill, *God's Englishman*, p. 272.

8 See *The Thomas Paine Reader*, ed. Michael Foot and Isaac Kramnick (Penguin, London, 1987), p. 19.

9 *New Statesman*, 11 March 1988.

10 Letter to the Bishop of Llandaff, reported in Christopher Hampton, ed., *A Radical Reader* (Penguin, London, 1984).

11 John Stuart Mill, *On Liberty and Considerations on Representative Government* (Basil Blackwell, Oxford, 1946), p. 136.

12 For an account, see Roy Jenkins, *Sir Charles Dilke* (Collins, London, 1958), p. 68.

13 Quoted in Nairn, *The Enchanted Glass* (Radius, London, 1988), p. 327.

14 The letters, papers and printed items from the collection of Bradlaugh's papers assembled by his daughter are now lodged at the Bishopsgate Institute in London.

15 Quoted in Hampton, op. cit., p. 561.

16 Quoted in Denis Judd, *Radical Joe: A Life of Joe Chamberlain* (Hamish Hamilton, London, 1977), p. 69.

17 See Frank Hardie, *The Political Influence of Queen Victoria* (Oxford University Press, London, 1935).

18 Quoted in Hampton, op. cit., p. 455.

19 Quoted in Hardie, op. cit., p. 210.

20 Quoted in Nairn, op. cit., p. 332.

21 Ibid., p. 326.

22 Jenkins, op. cit., p. 77.

23 See Harold Stannard, *The Two Constitutions* (A. & C. Black, London, 1949), p. 114.

24 Sarah Baxter, *New Statesman*, 18 December 1992.

25 Cited in Willie Hamilton, *My Queen and I* (Quartet Books, London, 1975), p. 107.

26 Laski made the charge in his 'The Crisis and the Constitution', Day to Day Pamphlets no. 9 (Hogarth Press, London, 1931), p. 34.

27 See Piers Brendon, 'Laughed out of Court', *New Statesman*, 18 December 1992.
28 The poll was reported in the *Sunday Telegraph*, 24 January 1993.

2 The Crisis of the Royal-state

1 Nairn, op. cit., p. 361.
2 Friedrich Engels, *The Condition of the Working Class in England*, quoted ibid., p. 204.
3 Walter Bagehot, *The English Constitution* (Fontana, London, 1963), p. 82.
4 See Philip Norton, *The Constitution in Flux* (Basil Blackwell, Oxford, 1982), p. 11.
5 Stuart Weir, 'This Sceptic Isle', *New Statesman and Society*, 26 February 1993.
6 Joe Rogaly, *Financial Times*, 24 November 1992.
7 See Dennis Kavanagh, *British Politics: Continuities and Change* (Oxford University Press, 1990), p. 38.
8 Reported in the *Daily Telegraph*, 5 November 1992.
9 Laski, op. cit., p. 31.
10 Kingsley Martin's *The Crown and the Establishment* (1963) is a reformist critique, and Percy Black's *The Mystique of Modern Monarchy* (1953) is primarily a psychological study.
11 Charles Petrie, *The Modern British Monarchy* (Eyre & Spottis-woode, London, 1961), p. 26.
12 *Evening Standard*, 13 August 1969; quoted in Andrew Duncan, *The Reality of Monarchy* (Heinemann, London, 1970), p. 285.
13 Duncan, op. cit., p. 335.
14 Quoted in Edgar Wilson, *The Myth of British Monarchy* (Journeyman Press, London, 1989), p. xi.
15 In the *Spectator*, 1968; quoted in Duncan, op. cit., p. 105.
16 *The Times*, 21 January 1992.
17 Ibid., Saturday Review, 1 February 1992.
18 *Daily Telegraph*, 24 July 1991.
19 *London Evening Standard*, 7 February 1992.

20 *Sunday Times*, 19 January 1992.
21 Phillip Hall, *Royal Fortune: Tax, Money and the Monarchy* (Bloomsbury, London, 1992), p. xv.
22 Andrew Morton, *Diana: Her True Story* (Simon & Schuster, London, 1992).
23 *Guardian*, 4 February 1992.
24 *Spectator*, 1 February 1992.
25 'The Public Mood and the Monarchy', *Daily Mail*, 24 November 1992.
26 *Financial Times*, 24 November 1992.
27 The Littlejohn Show, LBC, 27 November 1992.
28 *Independent*, 27 November 1992.
29 From a compilation of opinion by the *Independent*, 26 November 1992.
30 Alex Brummer, 'A Bicycling Monarch?', *Guardian*, 27 November 1992.
31 *Sunday Times*, 14 June 1992.
32 Reported in the *Observer*, 21 June 1992.
33 Reported on AM Alternative, BBC Radio 5, 20 November 1992.
34 Cited in Richard Tomlinson, 'Not So Happy Or Glorious', *Independent on Sunday*, 29 November 1992.
35 Ibid., Sunday Review, 5 April 1992.
36 *Sunday Times*, 14 June 1992.
37 On *Newsnight*, BBC TV, 3 January 1990.
38 Ibid.
39 Richard Stott, former editor of the *Daily Mirror*, quoted in the *Sun*, 4 December 1992.
40 See Wilson, op. cit., pp. 67–72.
41 Arnold Smith, *Stitches in Time: The Commonwealth in World Politics* (André Deutsch, London, 1981), p. 267.

3 The Cost of the Royal-state

1 For details of the Household, see Hall, op. cit., pp. 243–51; see also Hamilton, op. cit., pp. 254–7.

2 Figures from Wilson, op. cit., p. 49.
3 For a detailed assessment of the costs of the monarchy, see Hall, op. cit.
4 Ibid., p. xv.
5 Ibid., pp. 222–8.
6 Ibid., p. 251.
7 For a discussion of this controversy, see ibid., p. 186.
8 Quoted in Samuel Beer, *Britain against Itself: The Political Contradictions of Collectivism* (Norton, New York, 1982), p. 179.
9 Martin Weiner, *English Culture and the Decline of the Industrial Spirit (1850–1980)* (Viking, London, 1987).
10 Quoted in *Sunday Times*, 29 December 1991.1
11 John Morley, *The Life of Richard Cobden*, ii (1981), pp. 481–2.
12 Robert M. Adams, *Decadent Societies* (North Point Press, San Francisco, 1983), p. 94.
13 Correlli Barnett, *The Collapse of British Power* (Methuen, London, 1972), p. 24.
14 See A. H. Halsey, *The Decline of Donnish Dominion* (OUP, Oxford, 1992).
15 Shelley, *Complete Poetical Works*, p. 722; cited in Hampton, op. cit., p. 395.
16 Gordon S. Wood, *The Radicalism of the American Revolution* (Knopf, New York, 1992), p. 278.
17 Ibid., p. 286.
18 From 'The Queen: My Concern', *Mail on Sunday*, 24 January 1993.
19 Wood, op. cit., pp. 11–12.

4 The Wrong Constitution

1 Bagehot, op. cit., p. 82.
2 George Dangerfield, *The Strange Death of Liberal England* (MacGibbon & Kee, London, 1935), p. 41.
3 For a comprehensive account of public records secrecy, see Michael Roper, 'Access to Public Records', in *Open Government*, ed. Richard A. Chapman and Michael Hunt (Routledge, London, 1987).

4 Ibid., p. 17.

5 See Mill, op. cit., p. 141.

6 *Sunday Times*, 9 July 1987.

7 Robert Kilroy-Silk, *The Times*, 5 March 1988.

8 Anthony Sampson, *The Essential Anatomy of Britain* (Hodder & Stoughton, London, 1992), p. 62.

9 W. H. Greenleaf, *The British Political Tradition*, i: *The Rise of Collectivism* (Routledge, London, 1983), p. 196.

10 S. B. Crimes, *English Constitutional History* (Oxford University Press, London, 3rd edn, 1965), p. 67.

11 Quoted in Ivor Jennings, *The British Constitution* (Oxford University Press, London, 1966), p. 211.

12 A. V. Dicey, *An Introduction to the Study of the Law of the Constitution* (Macmillan, London, 10th edn, 1959), pp. 73–6.

13 Paine, op. cit., p. 221.

14 See David Cannadine, *The Decline and Fall of the British Aristocracy* (Yale University Press, New Haven, 1990).

15 *Observer* magazine, 8 March 1992.

16 Plumb, op. cit., p. 187.

17 Quoted in *Sunday Times*, 15 April 1990.

18 David Carlton, 'Modernising the Honours System', *The Radical*, September 1989, p. 15.

19 Lord Hailsham, 'Elective Dictatorship', Richard Dimbleby Lecture (BBC Books, London, 1976), pp. 12–14.

20 John Patten, 'Political Culture, Conservatism and Rolling Constitutional Change', Swinton Lecture, Conservative Political Centre (London, 1991), p. 15.

21 Ibid., p. 7.

22 George Walden, 'The Blocked Society', Tory Reform Group (London, December 1990).

23 Montesquieu, *The Spirit of Laws*, Book xi, Chapter 6; cited in Colin Turpin, *British Government and the Constitution* (Weidenfeld & Nicolson, London, 1985), p. 39.

24 Ibid.

25 Dicey, op. cit., pp. 39–40.

5 The Wrong Society

1 *Sunday Times*, 29 November 1992.
2 John Scott, *Who Rules Britain?* (Polity Press, Cambridge, 1991), argues that the social role became increasingly important as the political role slightly diminished.
3 Shirley Robin Letwin, *The Gentleman in Trollope* (Macmillan, London, 1982).
4 Robert Chesshyre, *The Return of the Native Reporter* (Penguin, London, 1987), p. 13.
5 Quoted in Duncan, op. cit.
6 *The Times*, 3 December 1992.
7 *Times Higher Educational Supplement*, 8 April 1988.
8 Malcolm Muggeridge, *The Infernal Grove* (Collins, London, 1973).
9 George Orwell, 'Such, Such were the Joys', *The Collected Essays, Journalism and Letters of George Orwell*, ed. Sonia Orwell and Ian Angus, iii (Secker & Warburg, London, 1968).
10 *The Times*, 16 November 1992.
11 D. Ryder, ed. *The Wit and Wisdom of Lloyd George* (Grant Richards, London, 1917), pp. 44–58.
12 Barry Penrose, *Conspiracy of Silence: The Secret Life of Anthony Blunt* (Vintage Books, New York, 1988), pp. 595–6.
13 For his discussion of the divine right of monarchy, see Michael Billig, *Talking of the Royal Family* (Routledge, London, 1992), pp. 65–7.
14 Ibid., p. 104.
15 Ibid., p. 103.
16 Ibid.
17 Richard North, 'An Insular Freedom to be Incompetent', *Independent*, 18 April 1992.
18 Billig, op. cit., p. 45.
19 *Evening Standard*, 21 September 1992.
20 Jonathan Israel, 'History in the Making', *Independent*, 28 December 1992.
21 *Sunday Times*, 25 October 1992.
22 *Sunday Telegraph*, 25 October 1992.
23 Rachel Johnson, *The Oxford Myth* (Weidenfeld & Nicolson, London, 1988), p. 148.

6 Fantasy Land: Illusions and Myths

1 *Independent*, 22 March 1992.
2 *The Times*, 16 November 1992.
3 *Today*, BBC Radio 4, 10 December 1992.
4 Interview with Anthony Clare for BBC Radio 4; reproduced in *The Republic*, vii, no. 2, winter 1991.
5 Reported in *Times Higher Educational Supplement*, 15 January 1993.
6 *Evening Standard*, 21 September 1992.
7 Stephen Howe, 'When the Sun did Set', *Times Higher Educational Supplement*, 13 November 1992.
8 Editorial, *Times Higher Educational Supplement*, 28 June 1988.
9 Billig, op. cit., p. 53.
10 Wilson, op. cit., p. 58, citing G. Bocca, *The UnEasy Heads: A Report on European Monarchy* (Weidenfeld & Nicolson, London, 1959), p. 210.
11 Wilson, op. cit., p. 57.
12 *Commentary*, August 1991.
13 See Justin Champion, *The Pillars of Priestcraft Shaken* (Cambridge University Press, Cambridge, 1992).
14 For a short discussion of this point, see Simon Denloon, *Independent*, 7 July 1992.
15 Quoted in Richard Tomlinson, 'Not So Happy Or Glorious', *Independent on Sunday*, 29 November 1992.

7 The Royal-state at Bay?

1 Nairn, op. cit., p. 9.
2 Barnett, op. cit., p. 593.
3 John Charmley, *Churchill: The End of Glory; a political biography* (John Curtis/Hodder & Stoughton, London, 1993), p. 13.
4 See Tony Benn, *Out of the Wilderness: Diaries 1963–1967* (Century Hutchinson, London, 1988).
5 Emily Crawford, *Victoria: Queen and Ruler* (Bristol Arrowsmith, London, 1903), p. 203.
6 See Maastricht treaty, Title V: 'Economic and Monetary Union'.

7 Ibid.
8 Ray Calamaro, 'An American Parallel', *Financial Times*, 13 November 1992.
9 See Maastricht treaty, Part 2, Article 8.
10 Maastricht treaty, Title 11.
11 Bernard Crick, 'The Fading Magic of Monarchy', *Guardian*, 6 February 1992.
12 *News at Ten*, ITV, 26 November 1992.
13 *The Economist*, 28 November 1992.
14 Kavanagh, op. cit., p. 37.
15 Samuel P. Huntingdon, *The Common Defense* (Columbia University Press, New York, 1961), p. 447.
16 See Anthony Jay, *Elizabeth R* (BBC Books, London, 1992).
17 *The Economist*, 12 December 1987.
18 Sue Townsend, *The Queen and I* (Methuen, London, 1992).

8 Letting Go

1 Jennings, op. cit., p. 211.
2 Peter Hennessey, paper given to the Radical Society, St Stephen's Club, London, 30 April 1992.
3 Quoted in Jenkins, op. cit., p. 71.
4 Hugh Massingberd, *Spectator*, 10 December 1992.
5 Bagehot, op. cit., p. 111.
6 Wilson, op. cit., p. 74.
7 Bagehot, op. cit., p. 85.
8 Jenkins, op. cit., p. 68.
9 See Hardie, op. cit., for a comprehensive account of Queen Victoria's political influence.
10 Lytton Strachey, *Queen Victoria* (London, 1918), p. 261.
11 Theo Aronson, *Victoria and Disraeli* (Cassell, London, 1977), p. 194.
12 Duncan, op. cit., p. 105.
13 A. Berriedale Keith, *The Constitution of England from Queen Victoria to George VI* (Macmillan, London, 1940), p. 9.
14 Hall, op. cit., p. 18.
15 Trowbridge Ford, *Albert Venn Dicey* (Rose, 1985), p. 241.

16 Duncan, op. cit., p. 222.
17 *New Society*, 3 October 1969; cited ibid., p. 225.
18 *Evening Standard*, 6 June 1969; quoted ibid., p. 225.
19 Ibid., p. 226.
20 Christopher Hill, *Milton and the English Revolution* (Penguin, London, 1977), p. 464 (my italics).
21 *The Times*, 10 October 1992, referring to a letter by the author.
22 HMSO, Royal Commission on the Constitution, report of October 1973, vol. i, p. 5.
23 See '"We, the People" Towards a Written Constitution', Federal Paper no. 13, Liberal Democrats, June 1990.
24 Bogdanor argued this novel case on a *Newsnight* programme, late in 1992.
25 Sampson, op. cit., pp. 61–2.
26 Cannadine, op. cit., p. 18.

9 A Dynamic Union

1 Neal Ascherson, *Independent on Sunday*, 8 November 1992.
2 *The Times*, 5 October 1992.
3 Gabriel M. Wilner, 'The Court of Justice', *The World and I*, December 1992, p. 39.
4 Maastricht treaty, Article 108.
5 Ibid., Article 109j.
6 Ibid., Transitional Provisions, Chapter 4, Section 1.
7 See 'Convergence Indicators for European Monetary Union', Table 10, in 'Unity and Diversity in Europe', Frankfurter Institut, September 1992, p. 10.
8 Maastricht treaty, Article 109j.
9 Editorial, *Independent*, 28 November 1992.
10 Frederick Jackson Turner, 'The West and Americans', *The Frontier in American History* (Holt, New York, 1921).

10 A British Republic

1 Liberal Democrats, '"We, the People"', Federal Paper no. 13.
2 Ibid.

3 Bagehot, op. cit., p. 119.

4 'The Constitutional Role and Duties of a Non-Hereditary Head of State', *Republic*, June 1992.

5 Quoted in Jenkins, op. cit., p. 73.

6 Judd, op. cit., p. 70.

7 Title 1, Article 3 of the Fifth Republic.

8 Title 11, Article 20, clause 2 of the Basic Law of the Federal Republic of Germany.

9 Maastricht treaty, Article 8.

10 These cases were reported in John Parry, 'European Citizenship', *The European Movement* (London, 1991).

11 Wilner, op. cit., p. 39.

12 Maastricht treaty, Title 6.

13 Quoted in Chapman and Hunt, op. cit., pp. 12–13.

14 This phrase was used by David Starkey in 'Let the Ancien Régime Beware', *Independent*, 21 January 1993.

15 Bernard Crick, 'The Fading Magic of Monarchy'.

16 *Eurobarometer*, Public Opinion in the European Community, Commission of the European Communities, June 1992, no. 37, p. 48.

17 Orwell, 'The Lion and the Unicorn', *Collected Essays*, ii, p. 6.

18 Nairn, op. cit., p. 128.

Index